(Then...)

est:

(Now: "The Landmark Forum")

Playing the Game*
The New Way

*The Game of Life

by

Carl Frederick

DEDICATION

To Mom

(who carried me in)

And

Mother Earth

(who supplied the necessary dirt and water)

Finally ~

To Werner Erhard

One of the ultimates in being-ness

FOREWORD

At the base of it all

This is nothing

But a lengthy letter

To myself.

And that simple truth

Puts the whole screed

In its proper perspective.

CONTENTS

EPILOGUE

INTRODUCTION

My purpose in creating this book is simply to assist you in getting everything that might be blocking you out of the way, so that you can proceed to win the games you have going. And before you start reading, I have a confession to make: it is that you already know everything in this tome. Not "some" of it – *all of it*. What I will do as we progress is create the space for you to put all the pieces together, in order that they begin to make some sense to you. But your life is your puzzle, not mine. It has been all along, and it will be for as long as you're around. I'm just a human being who happened to drop in to observe where it is that you're going.

So, from beginning to end, I want you to be the critic. If, at any point, you take a hard look at the words printed here and say to yourself: "This guy's off his rocker!" you should immediately junk the book. Stop reading it – you're wasting your valuable time. And whatever you do, don't let me lead you down any garden paths.

I submit that you've been letting other people tell you what to do with your life since it began. You've been running your life down a whole series of blind alleys that they created for you. And I'm telling you now that you're off your rocker for doing that to yourself.

As is evident from the title I've chosen, my experience has led me to see quite clearly that *LIFE IS A GAME*. Nothing more, and certainly nothing less. And, as you well know by now, all games have rules. For the purpose of this book, I'd like to call them "agreements." That is, you have chosen to sit down with me (the book), and play my game (read it.) And you understand clearly that at any point you can choose to upset the game board (close the book) and go away.

The agreements I want to make with you before you go on to Chapter One are as follows:

1. That you will make a conscious choice to really get involved with the message, and will simultaneously

discard as much as possible in terms of extraneous external things. What does that mean? To be perfectly clear, I want to be alone with you, in a quiet room. Don't read the book on a train, or at the beach, or anyplace where you might be interrupted. And don't pick it up if you've just experienced a problem in your life.

2. That you're going to be taking a long, careful and objective look at your life, to see if it's *working* for you. If you're not ready for that, please don't even bother to continue reading.

3. That you will read the book *only* when you're fully conscious. By "fully conscious" I mean: a) That you're wide awake. This is not a bedtime story – it's the game you call your life. b) That you've taken care of all your bodily functions and necessities before you sit down, and for as long as you choose to read at one sitting. If you 'have to go', that ends the session. Come back some other time. c) That you will abstain from all mind-altering potions, lotions and devices for at least twelve hours before you sit down to read. This includes aspirin, indigestion tablets, etc., as well as obvious things like

alcohol, marijuana, etc. You know what I'm talking about: don't cloud your head. d) Don't take any food into the room. My preference is also that you refrain from smoking, but this is not intended as an agreement, simply a suggestion.

4. Read slowly and methodically – let the words sink in. Kick them around thoroughly before you move on. Be certain whether they're true *for you*. If it takes you six conscious weeks to finish it on this basis, that's fine. This is not a one-night (book) stand, even though you might have thought that going in.

5. Get ready for the fact that, at times, you're going to want to throw away the book, hate me, and/or kick a wall. And I mean that you'll really be angry. Now I accept that. But you should be ready for it.

In summary: if you choose to explore your life and take a hard look at what's going on with you, let's get together. What lies ahead is just you, and you're such a perfect being that I'm going to enjoy every moment I get to be with you in your game. Nothing would give me more pleasure than seeing you playing the new way, then sharing that experience with you.

1. WHERE YOU ARE

Dear Abby:

Boy, am I ever pissed off at my old man. Here's what happened: I had this really big date set for Saturday night, so all week long I did everything right. I mean I cleaned up my room, took out the garbage, fed the dog, and even shined his shoes twice. Then, at the last minute, he refused to give me the car. Now isn't that unreasonable of him?

Signed, The Righteous Kid

Dear Righteous:

You are an unconscious ass. Why did you do that to you?

Love, Abby

Dear Abby:

Boy, am I ever pissed off at my boss. Let me tell you the story: For *six straight weeks* I put in fourteen hour days, plus Sundays, working on the Company's Five Year Plan. There wasn't a flaw in it when I finished, and I had a foreman at a tool and die company verify that. And it would have saved the Company $2.2 million the *first* year. But my boss only spent about 5 minutes glancing at it, then he just told me that "it wouldn't work." I didn't even get a chance to defend it. I think I would be perfectly justified to walk into his office and quit. What do you think?

Signed, The Frustrated Worker

Dear Frustrated:

You are an unconscious ass. Why did you do that to you?

Love, Abby

Dear Abby:

Boy, am I ever pissed off at my husband. Get this: Last Saturday he was out in the back yard, just putzin' around. I mean he wasn't really doing *anything*. And *anyone* could see that. He was just pickin' a few weeds and drinkin' a beer. Well, I asked him to come inside to watch the kids for ten lousy minutes while I went to the store, and he flat refused! He said that I should take the kids with me, which is exactly what I had to do, after a fifteen minute argument. Now wasn't he wrong?

Signed, I-get-no-cooperation

Dear I-get-no:

You are an unconscious ass. Why did you do that to you?

Love, Abby

Dear Abby:

Boy, am I ever pissed off at the world. I'm the quietest, most passive guy you'll find. I never cause any trouble for anyone. And in return I never *get* anything but the wrong end of the stick. My parents hassle me, the local fuzz hassles me, and my teachers hassle me. I think I should denounce my citizenship and move to Africa. What do you think?

Signed, Ready-To-Split

Dear Split:

You are an unconscious ass. Why are you doing that to you?

Love, Abby

So much for the examples. The point is that the people described are 1. REAL. You've seen and read about examples like these every day of your life. 2. UNCONSCIOUS ASSES. Unconscious because they really believe that the world, or the old man, or the boss, or the hubby, or whoever, is "doing it to them." The *fact* is they're doing it to themselves. .And that's precisely what makes them asses. 3. JUST LIKE YOU. Because if you're like 99% of the people I've observed in the world, you blame "it" on someone or something else, most of the time.

Take a moment, right now, and look at your life. And I mean really take a hard look. You have a remarkable ability to do that, which we will work on throughout this book. Just sit there and look at some situations where you know you've been right, and ultimately reasonable, but you didn't get what you wanted.

Now I want you to get the idea that the world you live in is NOT a reasonable place to be. In fact, very little about it is reasonable. So, if you're running your life in a reasonable way, the safest assumption to make is that you aren't going to get what you want very often.

And (no pun intended) there's a reason for that. It is that REASONABLENESS EQUALS RIGHTNESS. Those are states of mind, which equate to the way you run your life. And to be there with your life is the lowest state I can conceive of. Because when you're living there, you can literally end up losing all the games you set up, and the only thing you get out of them is knowing how "right" you were.

And the people you call your friends gather around and agree with you. You describe the game that you just lost, get them to agree that you were right, then they offer you a double martini on the rocks, as a consolation prize. And you swallow it, hook, line and twist of lemon. You ass.

Because the fact remains that you lost the little game, and (way back there in the far reaches of your head), you know that being right isn't the answer. You didn't get what you were after, and it's still frustrating as hell, even after all your "friends" have come to the emotional 'rescue'.

One final note: the ultimate in being right is to be *dead right*. That is, to be six feet under — literally — and the person who was wrong has absolutely no recourse with you. Oh, sure, he can come and stand over your headstone and cry wistfully, "I was wrong," but you aren't available for comment or compassion. So now he has to deal with that wrongness for the rest of his life. And somehow that pleases you too.

What I want you to get is the point of this discussion —
and you'll get it by taking a long, hard look at what's
going on out there in the world. Look at you, and at the
people around you. See how much time is wasted setting
up games, losing them, and then going around bitching
about the losses. For days. Weeks. Years. And yes, even
whole lifetimes.

Also, take special note of the fact that I said: "Games they
(and you) set up." Note that, because the fact is that no one
told you to create "I want the car for my date," or "I want
my plan to be accepted," or "I want my hubby to watch the
kids." No one ever created a game for you. You set them
up. You lose them. And I submit that you're an ass for
doing that to you.

Because I'm here to tell you that you can set up all the
games you want in life, then go about winning them. But
the winning isn't based on being right, or on being
reasonable. In fact, you're going to end up being
unreasonable as hell. But you get to win the games. And
that's the point. More on that later. For now, understand

one observable fact. It has to do with the contrast between animals and humans. Take a rat. Long ago, a brilliant psychologist proved that if you present a rat with 3 tunnels, only one of which has some cheese in it, the rat will explore all the avenues until it finds the cheese. And, after reinforcement, the rat will ignore all non-cheese tunnels, and only go down the one with the payoff. Then, if you take away the cheese, he will soon learn that it's gone, and will begin to explore all tunnels again, looking for the reward.

Human beings, in stark contrast, will go up a tunnel looking for whatever the "cheese" of the situation is, *never get any*, but they proceed to run up that same tunnel for a lifetime. And what's driving them is reasonableness, or rightness. That is, they say to themselves, quite logically: "I saw cheese go up that tunnel. It's got to be up there! I'll find it, dammit, if it takes me a lifetime!" So they get to spend a lifetime without cheese, but always being able to explain (to wives, friends, acquaintances — anyone who will listen) that they're up a very reasonable tunnel. And they find people to agree that the cheese really *belongs* up that tunnel. Those people are called really close friends.

If you're running your life up a tunnel (or a series of them) with no 'cheese' for you; if you're losing the games that you set up, you're beginning to get what I'm driving at: that running your life being right is pointless. And I don't mean that what you're doing is wrong; I simply mean that it doesn't WORK. And that's the criterion I'm going to use throughout this book — if it doesn't work for you — junk it. Drop it in the round file, because you're wasting your time. If what you see written here doesn't work for you, close the book, think of it as trash, and dump it. Go back to running your life the way you were. You don't need me (or anyone else) to inject more things into your life that send you up blind alleys. And that you can certainly agree with.

Now I want you to look at the incredible number of people who spend their entire lifetimes at "rightness." Being reasonable. They never get relief ~ they just get to bitch about it. Endlessly. They never face up to the truth of the matter, which is that they didn't get the results they wanted, and address that. Instead, they spend their lives talking about all the reasons they should have won the game.

However, as I observe things, there is usually at least one situation in the lives of most of us when we experience a jolt from our reasonableness. That is, the shock of the event moves us so quickly and forcefully that there isn't time to stop and bitch about it. We find ourselves caught up in it.

For example, take Mr. Dewright, a reasonable man with a wife, two kids, a dog, a station wagon, and a big house in Suburbia. He suddenly gets called into the boss's office and told that — for no reason that has to do with his ability — he's going to be on the curb at the end of the day. Reaction: "OHMIGOD! FIRED! FOR WHAT??????? I've been the most conscientious guy the company has seen. I mean, look at Smith: he just sits in his office all day, doing nothing. And Jones: he never shows up until 10:30! But it's me who gets the ax. What's wrong with the world/this company/me?"

This is the point of crisis where most people really begin to get a brief peek at the answer - and most do it without realizing what's going on. Because, when faced with the fact that being reasonable hasn't worked, they are then looking at two broad choices: A. Ending it all, by taking a leap from the Empire State Building, (or its hometown equivalent); or B. GRABBING HOLD OF THEIR BOOTSTRAPS. Looking at the situation, realizing that it wasn't right, but that NOTHING can be done to correct it, and moving on to a new situation. By not dwelling on the past, but going forward with the determination that he has to get another job, and be damn quick about it. He's got a family to be fed, plus a dog that doesn't get along very well without his Alpo, so *something* has to be done. NOW. And the *someone* elected to do it is Dewright. No one else really gives a damn. Oh, to be sure, his friends "appreciate" his unfortunate position; the employment agencies all say they'll go into action immediately, and his wife gets behind him.

BUT AT THE BASE ROOT OF IT ALL, DEWRIGHT'S COME TO THE UNDERSTANDING THAT HE HAS TO GET HIS ASS IN GEAR, AND FIND A SOLUTION. PRONTO!

And the job gets done. Three weeks (or three months) later, Dewright "finds" Corporation OK, where the people are "really nice" (reasonable), and the business is growing, and besides, it's closer to the house so he doesn't have to drive as far. So, he sits back and declares himself "alright" again.

It is absolutely unbelievable that people don't see the light at this point. What has happened is that they've used their natural talent to get through a rough situation, consciously pulled *themselves* up by the bootstraps, but then they throw off the responsibility for the future to the new Company: "Corporation OK is really going to take care of me. As a matter of fact, I don't know why I stayed at the old place as long as I did. I'm better off here."

Dewright should realize by now that nobody really cares about him but him. As I said before, people will say they do, but when it gets down to the nitty-gritty, they don't. And Dewright didn't really "need" them. The power to control what happens in his life is his alone. And if he brings things into his life that don't work, that frustrate him, that run him up blind tunnels with no cheese, he has the responsibility for that. NO ONE EVER DID IT TO HIM. HE DID IT TO HIMSELF. And the "how" and the "why" of it will unfold as you progress through this book.

For now, I want to expand upon what happened with Dewright. You will recall that he started off (in fact, ran his life) being reasonable. He did *everything* that a guy who is responsible would do — except that he got fired. Poor guy. The world's wrong — he's ok.

Here's what went on when Dewright got jolted out of his Rightness:

THE FISHTANK OF EFFECT

HELP

HOPE

FEAR OF WORSENING

DISASTER

CATATONIA

REASONABLENESS = RIGHTNESS

Operating his life from a base of reasonableness, he was suddenly hit with the fact that he didn't have a job anymore. His first reaction was Catatonic = he froze. In his head he couldn't comprehend what was going on. He was in a daze. From there, he moved up into Disaster. "What am I going to do *now*? This is a disaster! I have a family to support, and no job. Besides, I haven't put out any resumes. It's all over!"

Soon thereafter, he moved another step up, into Fear of Worsening. That is, he was in his third week of solving the problem and had several interviews, two of which "looked good," but got no firm offer. On the way home one night it occurred to him that *no one* out there was going to hire him and that he was on his way to becoming a derelict. On welfare. Accepting food stamps. And what will happen to the family? The dog? The station wagon? It was all falling apart and could only get worse. Being reasonable hadn't worked. "What the hell is the answer?" he mused rhetorically.

By now, you know the answer: it is to continue to be unreasonable — that, in fact, he's ok, and moving upward on his OWN POWER, and he'll soon see that. But our poor undeserving actor just keeps at it and gets up to: HOPE. Ah, he finally got an offer for only 10% less than he was making at the old joint and what's more, has three interviews set for next week. Plus, a friend in Kansas City has invited him to come back anytime, and told him there are four jobs in three companies to look at there. Ecstatic, Dewright declares: "There is some hope in the world!" Besides, he's basically covered. He has a firm job offer in hand.

You see: he's HELPED himself. Then he accepts the new job, gets elated about it, celebrates with the wife at dinner for $99.50, buys the dog 6 new cans of the best chow available, fills the tank of the wagon, makes the mortgage payment, and THROWS OFF THE RESPONSIBILITY FOR THE FUTURE TO THE NEW COMPANY. He says: "OK, now I've gotten myself this far, and I expect you to be reasonable (recognize my talents), and do *right* by me (keep me around, promote me, reward me for what I do)."

What a fool. Standing on the verge of the answer of his life, he abandons it all and returns to the lowest state around: REASONABLENESS= RIGHTNESS. Somebody can "do it to him" *again*.

Observing that fact about Dewright's behavior really pisses me off. Why am I angry? After all, the guy really did get to a better place, didn't he? The answer is — yes, *but*, the power he exercised in helping himself is one that he could have (and should have) stayed with. Because the next station upward in life is one that would have let him see clearly that he was a winner. And he walked away from it. Secondly, you're asking how it is that people go *forward* when they go through such apparently "horrible" states as catatonia, disaster, fear of worsening, etc. It sure as hell *looks* like they're going backwards to have to go through things like that.

And you're *right*. It sure does *look* that way. But the fact is that it ain't that way. Again, the reason (as if one were needed) is that just above HELP is a state of the human mind/condition that is unbelievable. But people don't see it, and that's the saddest commentary of all. It looks to them like they've reached the apex of human conditions. After all, he got help, and that's the time to return to running your life the way you used to ~ being reasonable. Isn't it???

No it's not. And we're going to explore what's up there at

the next level, in due time. For now, I want you to look at your life with the perspective of what happened to the guy who lost his job. Translate that in your terms, to *your* reality. See what happened. Look at your love life ~ a significant other who left you; a divorce. The death of someone you held very close — unexpectedly. Look at the last time you thought you would get the next promotion — but someone else got it. Look at the processes you used to get back to "normal." What you'll see is that you moved YOURSELF all the way UP to HELP, but then went ALL THE WAY BACK DOWN TO BEING REASONABLE; BEING RIGHT; THROWING OFF THE RESPON- SIBILITY FOR THE FUTURE ONTO SOMEONE OR SOMETHING ELSE.

By observation, I conclude that people who have to be "reasonable" or "right" about their lives, and are losing their games, are people who are putting on an ACT every day. They don't *see* it, of course, because if they could see it, they'd ditch the act, and do what *worked* for them. In the case of Dewright, we saw that being reasonable/right didn't work for him. He lost his job, and I call that not working. What *did* work was when *he* grabbed hold of his

bootstraps and pulled himself up to a better place.

And people who "put on" the rightness act are easy to picture: Envision someone who gets out of bed every day, spends two hours "getting ready," then hoists himself out over the very middle of the "Rightness River" (which, by the way, is more powerful than the mighty Colorado), and lowers himself into a frail canoe, which is floating freely in the treacherous rapids. He quickly reaches for the paddles, and begins to row frantically, in an effort to maintain balance, position, direction, and "getting somewhere." The only trouble is that he's ROWING AGAINST THE RIVER. And you know, as you watch him, that he's GOT TO LOSE. You can see that he isn't enjoying himself, that the river will *definitely* be there pushing long after he gives up, and that, anytime he loses a stroke, he also loses ground.

And the "Rightness River" is fed by a number of smaller

streams (of consciousness) that were — in turn — fed into the rower by a combination of folklore, instructions and "teachings" from his past. Things like:

— "You have to be better than other people; more successful."

— "You have to get married and be a good parent and buy a big house up on the hill."

— "You have to be like your father ~ aggressive and fast and powerful."

The list of "do's" and "don'ts" is *endless*. There are so many instructions and preachings from the past that we're using every day — unconsciously — that each of us has actually come to believe that *we* invented them. That they were ours all along. But the truth is that we simply made a decision (however long ago) to adopt these instructions as life purposes and proceeded to TRY to act them out. The only trouble is that human beings are bad actors. And to keep up the act is equal to rowing against the river. You're going to lose if you get yourself into a battle with a river. Forget it, there's no way that the river will "give up." It's got staying power that's way to hell and gone beyond the stamina of men, whether they recognize it or not. And finally, you must see that the river truly doesn't care whether you decide to ride with it, or whether you fight it by rowing in the opposite direction. It's just going where it's going, and it doesn't have a point-of-view about you, or about itself.

Another thing is happening when you're rowing against the river: it is that you've got your eyes set about two inches in front of you. (You damn well better, or you're not going to stay balanced.) And that means the flotsam and jetsam of the river is going to bang into you, thus creating more problems. They could, in fact, upset your whole applecart/canoe/life. And finally, you have absolutely no opportunity to take notice of what else is going on ~ that is, the other things that are floating by you in the river .~your span of vision is restricted to those paddles, the canoe, and staying afloat.

And you don't know where the hell you're going, because the answer is you're going NOWHERE. At best, all you can manage to do is stay even with the river. And that requires all the energy you can muster. Even you can see that one of the hardest things to do in the world is to maintain vigilance against the rapids, with an endless supply of water feeding them, and there you are, TRYING to go in the opposite direction. Really, it would be better if you junked your paddles, and just drifted along *with* the river. Even God knows you aren't going to "win" the battle you're fighting.

There are "rightness" acts all over the place for you to observe. Take the man in business who made a declaration to himself 20 years ago: "I'm going to be President of a big company someday!" Every day of his life he takes that act out into the river and rows like hell to try to stay even. Or, the young dude who decides that the establishment ain't for him, so he puts on the act that includes a beard, one ragged pair of faded jeans, and rows against the river. Or, the housewife who plays the game (acts out) getting into the social whirl by joining the Junior League.

What's your act? Take a careful look at that question, and stop reading until you have a clear idea of the act you're putting on every morning. See if it really is you.

Next, understand that there's a lot of ACT STANDARDIZATION in the world. By that I mean that the ticket for admission into the Aspen Act is a big sheep-dog and a Jeep ~ never a chopped and channeled Mustang. The business act requires a necktie and a Brooks Brothers suit. The commune act is one where there's no money and a street mutt. On and on: the Hollywood act, the Upper East Side New York act, the hometown USA act. And all of them have accompanying scripts for the actors to read.

GET THE NOTION THAT IT'S TIME TO DITCH YOUR ACT IF IT ISN'T WORKING FOR YOU. And how do you know if it's working? Simple: People whose lives are working have a rather sheepish grin on their faces ~ 95% of the time. They're getting what they really want out of their lives: the cheese. And, when you look closely at them, you know that they're not acting at all — that who you see is the real person, content with himself, going somewhere, WITH HIS RIVER. He's gotten out of the "Rightness River," and he's riding high. On top of his life. And he's not disturbed with himself, you, or the world. Nobody is "doing it to him." He's got control of his life, and it's readily apparent by his calmness, yet firmness, with the way he runs his life.

Are you there? I doubt it, because so few people are. But only *you* can answer that.

When you've cleaned up your act, and really find out who you are and where you really want to go, life consists of getting up every morning, taking your body out onto the River of Life, dropping into an innertube (with no paddles), and just coasting along, *with the river*. And I want to tell you that when you experience it, it's an amazing ride. For the first time in your life, you get to leisurely SEE what's going on all around you. And the process of living is easy as mom's apple pie ~ you're riding with the current.

I've come to New York City to write this book, and the observation of the actors in the rightness game here is astonishing. Cabbies who play it to the hilt ~ blow the horn at 1/10 of one second delays at a traffic signal. People who won't give you the time of day. Businessmen whose lives are so tightly screwed down (from all angles) that it literally takes them two days to recover if they miss a train. And if the Penn Central shuts down for a day, that does it to them for the rest of the month.

Can it be that I'm telling you the truth? Is it true that 99 and 44/100% of the people in the world are running their acts out into the Rightness River? Are you one of them? The answer is that you have to look at that and answer it for yourself. Based on experience, you probably are. I ought to know-. it was the way I ran my life for the first 33 years.

So, how did that happen? Why are you doing that to you?

Turn the page, and we'll look at you together.

2. HOW YOU GOT HERE

You were unconscious about your life, that's how you got here. And you are still unconscious.

Here's what's going on with you: get the idea that your life consists of nothing but one very long reel of videotape, with the past being represented by exposed film, and the present and future are still blank (unexposed). On this tape, *everything* that happens to you is recorded. And I do mean everything. It's a complete picture of all the sights, sounds, actions, tastes, smells, touches, feelings, considerations, decisions, judgments, rationalizations ~ everything.

It's all there. And you have the ability to play back every scene, if that's what you choose to do. Now you probably think there's a great deal about your life that you've "forgotten." Not true. It's all there on the videotape. And what's more, there are a lot of those pictures that you haul up and use for "reference" every day, whether you're conscious of using them or not.

Because this is the point where your *mind* comes into play. Get the idea that your mind exists for *only one purpose*: To save and replay those pictures of the past which it believes will make you *survive*. And by "survive" I don't mean just to keep your heart beating. It's much, much more than that. It includes things like whether it's ok for you to be sitting in the room you're in; whether it's ok for you to eat the food that's presented to you; whether it's ok for you to go 75 mph down the freeway, and so forth. In fact, your mind is what says it's ok for you to run your life *exactly* the way you're running it.

From a 'procedural' standpoint, what happens is that you find yourself presented with a situation wherein you have a choice: to do it or not to do it. At that point your mind enters the game, with the old pictures, to check you out. Then it issues a "GO" or "NO GO" decision, based on those pictures from the past. And every step of the way, as the event unfolds, your mind maintains the vigil, constantly checking to insure that you're ok; that you will continue to survive. That you're right, doing what you're doing.

GET THIS: YOUR MIND CANNOT LET YOU BE WRONG. TO DO THAT WOULD THREATEN YOUR SURVIVAL.

Now you can easily see how your mind comes into play in the 'major' incidents in your life, but I also want you to get that it interacts with you in *all* situations — even down to those that you would consider minor or inconsequential to your actual survival.

Take a light moment in life: you go to a nightclub to see a comedian. Take a look and see what a comedian actually does. If he's any good, *all* he's doing is RESHUFFLING YOUR PICTURES OF THE PAST. Because if he's talking about something that you can't bring up pictures for, he's making no sense to you, and to your mind that's equal to being wrong. So he's not funny. And you get up and leave, bitching about the cost and a wasted evening.

The point is that when you're unconscious about your life, you use your mind as the statistic. The "checker-outer," if you will. The *key* question, at this point, is whether your mind is accurate for you ~ that is, does it in fact serve up those pictures which actually have something to do with your survival, or is it screwing you up?

To make that analysis, let's use a real-life situation: Take the time you rode your tricycle down the street, didn't quite make it, turned over and crashed into a telephone pole. When you got yourself together, you discovered that your arm was scratched, that your head hurt, and you had a stomach ache, so you went home crying to mama. She fed you and told you it was ok; to be more careful the next time you ventured forth on your three-wheeler.

And the next time you get yourself into a situation where you *might* be hurt, your mind serves up the pictures of the headache and the stomach ache — AS IF THEY ACTUALLY HAD SOMETHING TO DO WITH YOUR SURVIVAL IN THE EARLIER SITUATION. So you get a headache and a stomach ache, and you get to "survive" once more. And your mind thinks the two events are actually *related.*

You see, the point is that your mind put you in the rightness game, and your mind keeps you stuck there. Your mind is screwing up your life by serving you pictures which, IN TRUTH, have absolutely nothing to do with your actual survival. Your mind seeks to make your life consistent, by serving you the same pictures when you get yourself into a situation which is even remotely similar to an earlier one. It thinks it's *helping* you by making your life consistent, even if it's consistently miserable, and not producing the results you want. Your mind gives you the APPEARANCE OF CERTAINTY, even if it frustrates you in the process (which it does). At least you get to be consistently *right.* That's why most of the world never moves out of the rightness game.

And don't get the notion that the pictures your mind serves up have to relate to traumatic or horrifying experiences. A woman once shared an experience with me that makes this point very clear: She was in her mid-thirties when I met her; and always had a terrific weight problem. At the time, she weighed about 200 pounds. When she looked at the pictures of her life, she saw what was happening at the time she was 6, 7, and 8. And the decision she made then about running her life. It was simply that she would get home from school, only to discover an empty house — no one at home. Her mother worked. Mom also saw to it that the maid came in regularly and kept the house spotless. Now this gal knew if she messed things up, she'd catch holy hell from her mother. So, because of the combination of "aloneness" (which gave her a knot in her stomach) and the fact she *couldn't* mess up the place, she ate. It calmed her stomach, and she made sure she didn't leave any scraps behind. THE DECISION TO EAT TO CALM THE "KNOT" WAS RUNNING HER LIFE FOR THE NEXT THIRTY YEARS. And, she was running her house the same way. Spotless. And the amazing thing to observe is that the moment she took a hard look at what was going on with her, the effect of it was immediately reduced. Within two weeks she had lost 10 pounds, by doing *nothing*. No diets. No calorie counters. All she did was look at what was going on with her every time her mind served up the knot in her stomach; the aloneness. Then she found she had a brand new, conscious CHOICE to make about eating. And most of the time she simply chose to skip it; realizing (finally!) that eating had absolutely nothing to do with surviving when she felt tense or alone. And once she realized this, she was quite able to deal with it. As a matter of fact, you should have *seen* the bright look of contentment and relief and aliveness on her face when she came to the point of realization that *she* had *control* of her weight. And no doctor or diet in the world was going to get her to that solution. She had the solution all the time.

As you take a hard look at your life and the lives of those around you, you will come to the realization that very few of us have had terrifying experiences which are running our lives. Au contraire: most of us were never gang-raped or threatened at gunpoint. Yet our lives are most definitely being run unconsciously, based on decisions we made long ago.

As incredible as it may seem, our minds are screwing up our lives. And we let that happen simply because we are unconscious about what's going on.

Another example: A lady friend was unusually cold and aloof. She had relationships, but was always on the "winning" side; very few people could get close to her; and *no one* ever got close enough to be able to hurt her. When she looked at that, she found that it all related to a decision she made back when she was very young. Her father was persistent in his position that "she could do it"; she could "stand on her own two feet"; that she should "get out there and show 'em!" The fact was that she couldn't — but she nevertheless made a decision (unconsciously) to let that stick with her and run her life. By the time she was 22, she had been in and out of four colleges. What happened was that she'd get there and just sit looking out the window, being cold and aloof. TRYING to stand up and show 'em. But she failed. Consistently. And when she looked and saw that those pictures were running her life, she had a conscious choice to make: whether or not to let them *continue* to run her life. She chose to ditch them, then went straight home to her father and cried her eyes out. She told the truth about what was running her life, and how it wasn't working. And he understood. In fact, he cried too. His little girl wanted to lean on him; she loved him. Ah, life is beautiful. But not when you're unconscious about it.

The TRUTH is that when you become conscious of the fact that your mind is serving up survival pictures from the past — and then you choose to take a hard look at those pictures — the effects of them will immediately *diminish*. And if you continue to look them square in the eye — to "tell it like it is" — the effects will *disappear* completely. Because you will then realize that you have a conscious choice to make: whether or not to let your pictures of a similar situation continue to run your life.

You have the opportunity to go into your life and validate what I've just said to you. Take a hard look at whatever you don't really like about you — then sit down somewhere all by yourself and tell the *truth* about it. No more lying to yourself; time to get on with it. And you should take whatever comes up. Don't push pictures out of your mind when they drift in. Take a look at them. Start by being conscious of the problem you're interested in, then re-run your videotape at the point the thing last happened to you. Since you're a physical being, it has to start at some point in your body. Where is it located? How far in? How far down? How big is it? What color? Is it moving? What thoughts do you have about it? What judgments?

Considerations? What do you see in the videotape pictures? Who was there? What were they saying? What were you doing?

Before you begin an exercise like the one described above, I want to acknowledge that you may be experiencing a great deal of fear with the prospect of taking that long, hard look at your life. It's almost as if you might wander back there and get permanently stuck. Or jump over the fence and go stark, raving mad. Let me reassure you by telling you something about you: the reason you feel that way is that you've been *acting* for one hell of a long time. And since you're still surviving (you are reading this book, aren't you?), you've got a strong and well-entrenched "buddy" to ditch while *you* take that look ~ your mind. You see, your mind has gone on all this time validating and revalidating the act you run every day. And you probably feel that if you ditched the act, the real you would be mean and ugly and all sorts of other "nasties" that have been lurking all this time.

The truth is that you are just you, and the effect of consciously re-running the videotape and looking at the pictures of your life is one of TREMENDOUS RELIEF. You finally get to go *through* issues (instead of sublimating them), and tell the truth to you about what was going on. And you can just be there, watching the tape run, looking at you. Get this: *You* are just *you*. You are *not* the event. *You* just went through it. You can go back and rerun the tape on all those issues you refused to deal with at the time they occurred and get them out of the way. Permanently. Only after you tell the truth will you come to the realization that you have total freedom to choose — to stop letting your old pictures run — and that's where you want to be.

At this point we begin the journey into your first episode of revelation. Look carefully at what I'm saying and *get the message*. Let it sink in. Kick it around. See if it's true for you. And don't let it go until you've really addressed it and KNOW where you are.

The *truth* is that if you're unconscious about your life, you're letting your mind serve up those pictures from the past which it *thinks* make you survive. And to survive EQUALS being right; being ok about everything that you do. And since your mind can only serve up pictures from the past, you're *living in the past*.

You're looking BACKWARDS, always trying to justify that what you've done is really alright. When you're not rowing against the Rightness River, you're standing on a rock out there in the middle, casting your fishing line backwards for pictures, trying to find reasons for your moves. You snag that picture on the tape, haul it up, find all sorts of reasons why you were right, and you try to make it ok that you *lost* the little game. Then you gather your friends around you, recreate the pictures for them, and get them to agree with you that you were reasonable ~ it was the world that was wrong. It *should* have gone your way. But the fact is that you don't have any cheese — you lost your own game. And you're an ass for doing that to you — unless you get your kicks out of being dead right, which is exactly where you're heading.

Now you get to see that you can't use your mind as the verifying statistic, for one simple reason: ITS PURPOSE IS TO MAKE YOU RIGHT (TO GIVE YOU JUSTIFI-CATION) AND *NOT* TO MAKE YOU WIN. Because it thinks that by being right, you get to survive. The problem is that in life you end up with only one of two things: A. RESULTS; or B. THE REASONS YOU DIDN'T GET THEM. Your mind is resistant to the truth, because the truth simply IS, that's all. It doesn't need reasons; it doesn't have to be right; it's just the truth. Period.

Let's look at an example: a salesman who has just emerged from a call on one of his accounts. I submit to you that he can only have one of two things: 1. RESULTS (he made the sale) or 2. a whole bunch of REASONS why he didn't close the deal. Also, notice that when he has *results*, no one asks for the reason(s) why. Results can be left alone — they don't need any reasons. But your mind is resistant to that notion. And that's because your mind desperately wants things to be like they WERE, not like they ARE. Your mind cannot create anything, it can only *imitate* what was. And that means you're standing on that rock, fishing in the past, trying to justify what was. And there's one other thing you're doing: wasting more valuable time.

Maybe someday the real you will become convinced that being right doesn't really represent an answer. You'll get sick and tired of "surviving" while losing your games. If that begins to gnaw at you, you'll begin to move, in accordance with the chart I outlined earlier. You'll go into catatonia, then disaster, etc. And when you get through hope, you would typically seek help. From your *friendly* psychiatrist. You're probably one step ahead of me, but you know where I'm taking you. Yep, the shrinks of the world make $200 every 30 minutes *by agreeing with you.* They're just expensive friends, who help you find the right pictures on the videotape, take a long and hard look at them, and then make you *right* about them. In fact, they help you drive yourself even deeper into the mud next to the pictures, by having you *analyze* what was going on. And this process keeps you firmly anchored in the past, fishing like hell to stay ok about what happened then. The nice part of their job is that it represents a fantastic security blanket — for them — because the past really piles up, fast. At some point you might get to the place where you can start to fish in the experience/pictures of him and you. But you're still in the past.

And you're still the same old unconscious loser, because

you're anchored on that rock, casting your line backwards, and looking backwards, too. That means the present is going by without you knowing about it consciously. And just when you least expect it — BAM! — you get hit right between the eyes with another big, ugly piece of flotsam or jetsam from the river. Remember that the River of Life never stops flowing. It's just like the tide; it was here long before you arrived, and it'll be here long after you fade away. And it really doesn't give a damn whether you try to push it around, or whether you choose to get in an inner tube and simply go along for the ride. The River of Life goes on.

As you can now see, one of the biggest problems with your life is simply that you're facing the wrong way. You're looking backwards, trying to justify what you've already done. And I'm here to tell you that if you manage to accomplish nothing more than TURNING AROUND — facing forward, looking at the present and the future, you'll be well on your way to winning the game. You'll see clearly that you have control of your life, and for the first time, you'll *know* where you're going. You'll be able to dodge 95% of the flotsam and jetsam; then really be impressed because it was only you who got you out of the way. Your life will become free and easy – EFFORTLESS – because you'll be riding *with the river*. You'll also discover that you end up with the cheese; you get to win the games you set up. Without *trying* to win them.

If you're ready to turn around, we can begin our journey upward together.

3. WHAT'S ABOVE HELP?

Just a short while ago, I told you about the condition your
life is in right now: running from the lowest station called
REASONABLENESS/RIGHTNESS and, for some people,
moving upward through HELP. You should know that
while HELP is indeed a higher condition of life than
REASONABLENESS, it is still in the same fishtank. And
that muddy tank is one I call the *FISHTANK OF EFFECT*.
Which is to say that all the fishies in the tank are not AT
CAUSE with their lives, but rather are *AT EFFECT*. And
no matter where you are in the tank, you are in a negative
position. The world is doing it to you. You're running your
life reasonably, which you can readily and completely
explain to anyone who'll listen. BUT YOU'RE LOSING

THE GAMES YOU SET UP. If there's some "hope in sight," that means it's coming from someone other than you. And when you get help, you get it from someone else. So that if he ends up not really helping you, *he* did it to you. It's not your fault. You were alright all along.

There's another amazing thing to observe: it is that most people who are in the rightness game describe their lives as if they were on a giant roller coaster. And they can see that the car (called life) is running downhill. They acknowledge that freely; noting that it's been that way "for as long as I can remember." But (and this is the absolute height of stupidity) they continue to HOPE LIKE HELL that they'll soon reach the bottom, and then the trolley of life will be carrying them upward for once. You've heard the story: "I've been the reasonable guy all this time and have been dealt dirt. Surely I have some of the good life coming at some point, don't I?"

The answer to that question is an emphatic NO! You've got nothing coming but more of the same. You're stuck in the Fishtank of Effect, and unless you see the light and choose to leave it, the world will continue to "do you wrong," and you'll end up being dead right. But a loser, all the same.

So how do you get out of the stagnant tank you're stuck in? Well, let me begin by telling you that the "light" I mentioned is a very thin shaft indeed. Not many people see it in the Fishtank of Effect, but it does shine there. And when you get right under it and look up it, you can't see anything at the other end. That's why 99.9% of the people in the world decide that they aren't going to go up there and look around. They'd rather go back down to rightness and run their lives that way. At least they *know* what's there.

And if you choose to start up the shaft of light, you will see that there is, in fact, nothing there. It's just there, and you're just passing through it. You're on a little trip up through the light beam, toward the source, which you can't see. Imagine that you are really in that shaft of light — right now — and begin to get the feeling that it's totally alright for you to be there. Even though you don't know what's coming. What you have is the confidence that wherever you're going has to be better than the rancid fishtank that you've been stuck in all this time. And sure enough, you're right.

Because the first thing you'll find at the end of the light beam is a condition of life you've never experienced before — it's POSITIVE — and it starts with ACCEPTANCE.

You're going to have to work at getting this, because by acceptance I mean TRUE ACCEPTANCE OF EVERYTHING that goes by you in your life. That is to say, the PAST IS GONE, AND THERE ISN'T A BLOODY THING YOU CAN DO TO CHANGE IT.

Get that: ***THERE IS ABSOLUTELY NOTHING YOU CAN DO ABOUT THE PAST.***

You can look at it, but there is no way you can change it.

If you can change or control *anything* in your life, it is nothing but the present and the future. The minute something goes onto the videotape and down the river into the past, get the idea of letting it alone. Just let it be there.

For example, if at some point you decide to ditch this

book, what purpose is there in going around bitching about what a stupid story it was or what a crazy author I am? If you do that, all you'll be doing is wasting more of your valuable time trying to change what was. Sorry, baby, you can't get there from here. All you can end up with is rightness, plus all the accompanying reasons.

What is true acceptance? And how will you know when you're running your life in that condition? The truth is that only you can know. But try this as one criterion: when something happens that gives you every reason to be damn mad - and I mean really angry - consciously choose to stop for just a split second before you let your mind serve up the vengeance pictures. Take a look at the event. Experience the truth: that there isn't a single thing you can do to change what's happened — it's already locked into the videotape called the past. Now you're faced with the future. What is your purpose in going into vengeance? Are you simply chasing the tape to try to correct it? And when you get at the truth for you about the matter, go ahead and do whatever it is you choose to do. And then let it alone. That's acceptance.

And when you get to TOTAL acceptance, you'll find that living is really an exciting trip. And it'll be that way simply because you will have turned your life around. You'll be facing forward for the first time, looking out there in front of you for what's coming, not backwards at what went by. And when you get there, you'll be so impressed with you and your new life that you won't be the same for a couple of days. Maybe a week. Maybe never.

Because at that point you will have elevated your life to a totally new place, with a totally new orientation: it's one I choose to call the "CLOUD OF CAUSE." And it's up there that you will finally get to see exactly who it is with the "control stick" over your life. That's right~ *you* have it. Once you really get that, you'll find that you can just sail around up there on the cloud, getting happier and happier about you. And the sheer delight will come from just one simple fact — you'll *know* that you have control over the big game you're in — and you'll also know that you've had it all along, but just never acknowledged it before.

And the condition of Total Acceptance is just the

beginning of the new life you'll discover when you get to the Cloud of Cause. What'll happen is that you'll get to another condition, one that's just above Acceptance. It's called RESPONSIBILITY. And again I mean total and complete responsibility for everything that comes into your life. Everything. No exceptions.

Here's an example to bring Total Acceptance and Responsibility into clear focus: when you were unconscious about your life, you were simply turned the wrong way, looking backwards, trying to fish in the pictures of the past to justify the moves you made. And, over time, you had to handle so much exposed videotape that it ended up all over the place, with no take-up reel, and was a genuine mess. Then you got disgusted, so you chose to forget trying to sort it out, and instead became determined to find out what the source of it was. So you just headed up the tape ~ climbing like crazy to find out where it was coming from. Before long, you noticed a hatch door, and the tape was coming down from there. And you opened the hatch, only to discover that you were in your head. You looked around and saw that there were a couple of things up there: first, a big director's chair ~ it was empty. And next you saw a huge roll of unexposed film, all neatly racked on a roll. Finally, you realized that the film was exposed as it rolled by your eyes.

With this new knowledge, you have a choice: do you sit in the director's chair or not? And if you sit down, you'll find that the chair was made just for you. Comfortable and relaxing. Then you'll come to the stark realization that you really are the director~ that's what you wanted to be all along. You'll really get excited when you point your eyes forward and actually see what it is that you'll be filming. And the prospect of returning to where you were~ being inundated by used film; confused by it all, frustrated~ is one that you immediately reject. That's pure insanity. You choose to sit right where you are~ directing.

And now you get to see that I've just "done something" to you. A rough equivalent would be a picture of you and me in a luxurious 165-foot yacht, out in the open seas, going about 30 knots, and I'm steering. Suddenly, and for no apparent reason, I jump overboard and yell as I go: "She's all yours!" And the ship I just abandoned is the one you call your life. So now you've got several choices. You can spend the rest of your life looking backwards at the point where I jumped, shaking your clenched fist at me. You can refuse to take the wheel and go below decks and cry, or drink some booze, and hope like hell that the boat (mysteriously) finds a safe harbor.

OR YOU CAN ACCEPT THE FACT THAT I'M GONE AND TAKE THE WHEEL: STEER THE DAMN THING!

And you better get the notion that I don't really care what you do. It's all yours. And if you get with it, you'll see that what you really wanted to be is just what you are ~ the captain. You'll find that it's really a breeze to be at the helm. And before long, you'll realize that you actually do know where you're going. Hot Damn! And, of course, there's no one to blame if you don't get there but you. You really get conscious about what you're doing because you don't want to wreck the ship —say "cheese", it isn't every day that someone throws you the wheel of a 165-foot yacht and says, "Take over." That's a valuable piece of goods you have control of. You don't let it drift anywhere ~oh, no, you watch where it's going. You're the captain, and, as every sailor knows, the captain is responsible for everything that happens to the ship. And not *partly* responsible, TOTALLY responsible.

Now, as you look ahead to responsibility, you'll see that there are many events/conditions/situations, etc., that come into your life where you can clearly see a direct line of cause and effect between you and what happened. And you'll find that you're ready to take responsibility for those things. But there are other circumstances where you'll look and declare truthfully to yourself that you can't see any connection between you and the end result. So how could you be responsible?

Here's what to do about that. First, take my word for it, you were at cause in the matter, no matter what it was. Second, just sit there and be totally willing to accept responsibility for whatever it was. That *willingness* to be responsible is the key. And when you go through the experience of being willing to take responsibility for everything in your life, you'll intuitively understand what I mean. And that experience will lift you even higher on the Cloud of Cause.

Now I want to acknowledge that as you look ahead from where you are to the Total Responsibility I'm talking about, it appears that you'll be carrying the weight of the world around on your shoulders. Again, the only way to know is to experience it yourself. Don't let me (or anyone else) lead you up any more tunnels with no cheese. Go through it and see for yourself. Then, if it doesn't work, pull the plug and sink it.

My experience with total responsibility is absolutely unbelievable. First, you must understand that there are two sides to the coin. One side is positive. That is, you get to take responsibility for all things that go exactly as you want them to. That side has turned into 95% of my life, and I get to take responsibility for it, all the time it's happening. Then there's the negative side. You'll find yourself filming a massive traffic jam on the freeway and ask yourself: "Why did I do this to me? What am I getting out of it?" You'll find yourself driving around looking for a parking space for 20 minutes and ask, "Why did I do this to me?" You'll discover a long line of people at the bank and ask, "Why am I doing this to me?" And so on.

What will absolutely astound you is the fact that when you're willing to be responsible for everything that happens in your life, you'll simultaneously discover that you really don't want to be hassled — and it's then that the hassles will actually begin to *disappear.*

Now, when it first began to happen with me, I couldn't believe it. I called it luck. But you must understand that the opposite of luck is un-luck, and that translates to someone else/something else "doing it to you." Nobody ever did anything to you. When you get that, it'll elevate you to an even higher place on the Cloud of Cause. *Your* cause, coincidentally.

Now I want to relate the experience of the next condition available to you, up there on the Cloud of Cause. As you begin to live the fullest life in the condition of responsibility, you will encounter two questions: "Who am I?" and "Where am I going?"

The answer to "Who am I?" is that you are simply the human being with the choice to make. Note that I said "choice" and not "decision." My definitions are as follows: when you choose, you know that your range of options is *limitless.* That is to say, if a person approaches you with two items and demands: "Pick one," you understand that you can always choose to deal yourself out of that game *without* making the selection that the person wanted. When you "decide" is when you think there are only the two options he has presented, and that you must decide on one of them.

The important thing to note is that in the game of life you don't have a choice between choosing and not choosing. You must make some choice and then live with the consequences. (Or you can choose to take a header off the Golden Gate Bridge, but that, too, is a choice. You just don't get to live with it for very long.)

Acknowledging that basic truth will bring you to a new condition on the Cloud of Cause, one I call RECOGNITION.

Basically, it's the recognition that when you've got the camera out there looking in front, you won't always know exactly what you'll be filming in the future. Now, that recognition carries with it another condition called UNCERTAINTY. That is, when faced with a choice, you must choose, and you know that. But, how will you know if the choice is appropriate? What you will find is that your life is running so well that you'll always be willing to make a choice, that you will always choose, and it will be ok. The truth is that you will intuitively know which choice to make, will be responsible for that choice, and will totally accept its consequences. And the absolute truth is that there is no certainty on this earth outside yourself.

But where am I going? What's my purpose in life? I must defer that question to a chapter in the book that lies ahead. For now, all you need to know is that you're getting there. Of that much you can be absolutely certain.

Now I want to deal with the highest condition I can conceive of in the game called life. Just a notch above Recognition is a space called SOURCE. And when you get there, your inner glow will capture all those who come within five miles of you. This is the condition wherein you look, see, and KNOW that you alone have created the game called life, and everything that it contains for you. You know that you set it up ~ including all the rules~ and then go about winning or losing it.

And at that point you'll discover that you never wanted to be a loser. So you're a winner. All the time. And the unbelievable part is that *no one loses*. Life is incredibly beautiful when you live that experience. The 'bonus' is that it's really out there for you! All the cheese. And now you're ready to see how to create all the cheese from the people in your game.

4. HOW TO GET ALL THE CHEESE IN LIFE

OR

"HOW UNREASONABLE CAN YOU BE?"

We have seen quite clearly that unconscious people (i.e., the majority) in this world are living their lives down there in the negative place called the Fishtank of Effect. Most of them, in fact, are at the absolute bottom of the tank, wallowing around in RIGHTNESS. Boy, are they reasonable about their lives! And now you know where that leads: straight down into a statement from the afflicted that goes, "Damn, I don't understand. Look at all the reasons I should have gotten ____. Why, I _____ and

I _____, and I even_____ _____ But I still lost out. Somethin' is definitely wrong with the world!" You can fill in the blanks~ you are intimately familiar with the situations and experiences, because that *was* your life.

What I want you to get from this discussion is the fact that the people who are stuck down there at Rightness are *really* stuck. I mean they firmly believe that they're right; they're genuine when they want to spend the next two hours having you listen to the tale of woe (and then agree with them). Similarly, people who approach you with a point of view different from yours really believe that theirs is correct; yours is in error.

Get this: any person who is floating around unconsciously is *truly unconscious*. His mind is serving up pictures which are intended only to make him "survive," which means he must be right at all costs.

And ~ very importantly ~ in getting what you want from people, you must get to the point of acknowledging and accepting the genuineness, perfection, and the hard reality of what they believe.

In getting what you want from them, you must not try to change the fact that they're right. Oh, no, you just acknowledge it and leave it ALONE.

In fact, one of the key guidelines in getting your life to work is so simple it'll stagger you. It is to:

GIVE UP BEING RIGHT.

TOTALLY AND COMPLETELY.

Let the other guy be right; you go on and win the game that you set up. And please note that I didn't say "Give up what you really want out of life." I simply said to give up being right about it.

You can go out and validate this 50 times in a day. It makes your life work, and you will (naturally) get higher and higher as you see what's happening with you. The following experiences which I will share with you offer some tangible validations. Since they are so common, you will also find that some fit your experience to the letter. How did they come out for you? Did you win the game you set up? Would you now?

Life situation: I dialed Information on the phone and asked the operator for two numbers. She promptly informed me that she couldn't do that: it was "against Company Policy." My reply: "Fine, I understand that. But you see my problem is that I'm in a hurry to make an appointment, and I'm running late. How can we solve that?" Result: She gave me both numbers with no further questions.

Life situation: A friend walked into the airport in San Diego with a huge lamp which he had just bought in Mexico. It was unwrapped. The ticket agent took one look and announced flatly: "You can't take that aboard, and I can't check it if it's unwrapped." My friend's reply: "Fine, I understand that. But I have a problem in that I have to make that plane. How can we get this lamp to Los Angeles?" Result: The agent smiled broadly, offered to wrap the lamp and send it to L.A. on the next plane. It was delivered to my friend's home four hours later.

Life situation: I was called into the President's office with another gentleman, and both of us were told that the budgets couldn't carry us any longer. My associate flew into a nasty harangue, insisting that he had been "done dirty," banged his fist on the boss' desk and stormed out of the office, slamming the door behind him. I looked the Pres straight in the eye and calmly said: "I understand your position. As a matter of fact, I've been working with the budgets so I know how tight they are. But I have this problem — I have no money and no car. How can we solve that?" Result: I left his office with one year additional use of my Company car, all expenses paid, and a three-month cash advance on a part-time consulting contract which I suggested to him.

More examples will follow because I really enjoy sharing experiences which illustrate clearly how a person (even you) can get his life to work for him. But, right now, I want you to look at these experiences and really get what was going on. The first thing you'll see is that you have a choice to make when confronted with someone trying to make you wrong. You can choose to make him or her wrong, and that will get you into a dandy argument, without fail. Example: I could have 'lashed back' at the Information Operator with something like, "Ah, c'mon. That's a lot of nonsense. If you don't give me the second number, I'll just have to dial 411 again and get it. So you might as well give it to me now!" And I probably wouldn't have gotten it. But I would have been right. I mean, "What the hell do those operators do all day besides sit on their butts?" And the policy of one number at a time is just plain stupid. Well, you get into a ten-minute argument — I'd rather have the cheese, thank you, and that's exactly what I got. In record time. Without any problem at all.

As a matter of fact, you have another opportunity to get people to assist you in getting more cheese faster than you ever dreamed. All you have to do to get there is return a thing called Recognition, after you've won the game you set up. That equates to: "Operator, I understand your Company's policy is not to give out two numbers at once, and I really appreciate the fact that you've done it for me. Thank you."

Or, when I left the boss's office, I said, "I understand that money is really tight, and I really appreciate what you've done for me. Thank you." And I *meant* it. After all, I got what I wanted.

As you look at life, you'll see that there is so damn little return Recognition being dealt out by people to others that if you start the practice (when you win your games), you will leave behind a group of loyal *followers*. People who would go out of their way to help you get what you want the next time you run into them. They'll look at you and say, "Hey, he understands me." And you do. Then you get to derive even greater satisfaction when you see the glow in their eyes. Ah, life is great ~when it's working for you!

When your life begins to turn out this way, you will see that the easiest thing to do when you approach someone with your game is to deal it to him from his vantage point. And that lets him do what you want right away, without offering any argument. Just get behind him for a minute. Look and know where he is, then start from that position.

Example: I approached the Creative Director at the Company I used to work for and wanted some artwork in a hurry. I opened with: "Mary, I'm looking at your desk, and it's apparent that you have a million things to get out. But I have this special job that I need by 3 PM. Can you help me?" Result: She returned the artwork two hours later, at 1 PM.

Experience the results you get when you open with people

by getting into their moccasins, letting that be alright with you, and open the conversation from that position.

Let's look at you — and a situation you might find at work: you want a raise, you feel justified, and you haven't heard a word from your boss in 14 months. Since you already know how to get into an argument with him on the subject, I'm going to skip that and move on to ask you to look at this example: "Boss, I understand that the pressures here are really heavy, and that you've got a lot of things on your mind. But my problem is that I need more money, and I haven't had a review of my salary in 14 months. Can we talk about that?"

There are other games which you will insist you did not create, but nevertheless find that you must face. Like when someone comes to you and insists, "You have to do this for me!" The situation is no different. What you should do is simply take that split second to look at what's being presented, choose whether you will play or not, and then state your purpose, without making the other person wrong.

Life situation: The boss approaches you at 5 PM (your

quitting time) and shouts: "You have to work overtime because Jones didn't show up!" You look and choose not to do that and then reply: "I understand that you really need someone to work overtime, and I would normally do it, but I can't tonight because I've made plans that I simply can't break."

Now what you must do is go out and seek validations for you. Perhaps you have looked at these examples and disagree with their workability. There's no bullshit here. What's happening is that you're missing one very important element: that of being there and experiencing the situation. Because there's an *invisible* force at work which is difficult to describe to anyone — that of the PLACE FROM WHICH ONE COMES WHEN HE MAKES A STATEMENT. By that I mean that you're not flailing around unconsciously anymore. You've stopped, looked, chosen, and stated where you are. And people can see that you really come from the "yes" or "no" that you deliver. They can see that you're not a person to be manipulated. You mean what you say. And they're still not wrong.

There's something I want you to consciously test: it is my

theory that 50% of your life will work if you simply give up being right. For most people, its 80% or 90%. But just go out and look for 50%. That's not a bad average, and the actual results will amaze you.

Because there will be a couple of additional things going on with you. One of them will be that you will discover that your life gets very *consistent*. When you say something, you mean it. People get to know that over time. If someone brings you a game, and you choose to play with them, simply say, "Fine, I'll be glad to do that." And then do it. Don't bitch about it when it's over. You allowed the game to take place, and now it's just back there on the videotape. Accept it. It happened. It was. It's gone. You can't change it.

Another thing you will discover it that you'll have more time on your hands when you avoid problems. As you look at your unconscious life (before you started reading), you routinely got into 15-minute arguments about whether or not you were going to do things. Now you'll find that you save all that time. And, if you were responsible before, you are really responsible now. You get to "have all the cheese" and really take pride in you. You're winning games. And there's nobody left behind in an upset state. You know, life is absolutely beautiful when it's working!

Something else is going to dawn on you before too long, and I want to address it now. It relates to the power that you will have over your life. That is, as your games begin to work exactly as you want them to, you will have occasion to stand back and question the ethics of having all this go right for you. And you'll be correct in addressing it. Because there is an unbelievable (almost incomprehensible) amount of power and control that you will be exercising over your life. And that power will inevitably involve the lives of others. You might get the notion that you're actually manipulating others. And you'll be right again. And at that point, you'll have another choice to make: whether to be the manipulator or to return to being manipulated. Because that's *all there is*.

History supports the massive power behind giving up being right. It's been called *surrender*. Notice I did not say 'succumb'. Take a look at Japan and Germany. At this writing, their currencies are the world's standard. The

Japanese already own everything that's worthwhile in Hawaii and are now moving in on California. And you already know the country of origin of the largest selling imported car. Well volks, both those countries said, when the Second War game ended: "Hey, you guy are right. We give up! Here, take all our guns and ammunition. But you've left us with this problem in that you've bombed the hell out of us, and we have to rebuild. How are we going to solve that?" And the U.S.A. played their game! While Britain (our ally in that one) didn't get enough money to resurface Piccadilly Circus (which was blown to bits, incidentally.) Ironic as hell, isn't it?

Now let's take a look at one of my favorite subjects: the fair sex. Some of them (the smart ones) have had the secret all along. It's typified by the following example: Hubby comes home from work. Now we all know that he's the cornerstone of the family; the power, the strength. He finds a statement from Lord of Lords Department Store, which indicates that he owes $879 for a couple of dresses, some shoes, and two new bikinis for you-know-who. And is he ever pissed off: "What the hell is this? Don't you know we're in hock to our eyeballs now?" Sure she does. And she also knows not to question the wisdom of the king of the household. So she replies, softly: "I know, honey. You're right. I do spend much too freely. But I just wanted to look nice for you when we go to the Virgin Islands next month." Now what can the old man say? Case closed (until next month, when she plays the same game again). And notice that nothing was said about the creation of the Virgins vacation, and who set that up.

Now take a cold, analytical look at what happens to games when you give up being right about them. The logical implications will literally shatter you. Because it is transparent that what you're doing is simply acknowledging that what they're saying you can't do/have is totally ok with you. But then you turn around and do nothing but repeat the request. For the same thing. And you end up getting it.

What's going on there? Simple: One word or phrase like, "Fine. I understand that." Or, "Yes. I got that," serves the purpose of CLOSING THE RIGHTNESS DOOR FOR THAT PERSON. And then he's open to deal with your problem. That is, the person you're confronting can only deal with your problem if his mind tells him he's going to survive. And you've told him nothing more than his present position is perfectly alright with you; you're acknowledging NOTHING BUT THE FACT THAT HE'S GENUINELY WHERE HE IS. He then concludes (unconsciously) that he will survive. And now that his situation is OK, you're left with a problem, which you deal right back to him for solution.

Said another way, you create a "safe space" for the other person when you let him be right. It's as if he peered out from behind a large, heavy door of defense and stated that "this is my position." You acknowledge him and tell him to come out ~it's ok~ "Don't be afraid to have that position." It's alright with you for him to be where he is — to say what he's saying. And he doesn't have to defend himself or make himself right about where he is. You close the rightness door simply by saying, "Fine. I understand that."

Now if you were being reasonable about your life, you'd say, "That's dumb," or "That's acting like a kid." And let me be the first to acknowledge that you'd be right. But it also happens to be the key to getting what you want out of life. And what you want out of life is what you want out of life. Nobody on this earth gets your ideas and goals and objectives and purposes for you. You're setting it all up. And it's one large game, with a never-ending series of mini-games. And the only choice you have is whether you want to win or lose. What I've done is simply to let you in on how to win. If you now choose to lose, that's your choice. And it's your life. Nobody else really cares how it comes out for you. They've got their own games to worry about.

So, to get people to assist you in getting your cheese, you have to be unreasonable. You have to recognize that you're creating problems for people when you create games for them to play (and let you win). Because from a logical standpoint, nice guys don't hand their problems to others. You would certainly never hand your problems to your friends, would you? Well, the fact is that you were constantly handing them problems — but those problems related to agreement and rightness. And they solved them for you — their valuable time was spent listening to you and agreeing with you. So, it seems that what we're left with is an issue of semantics.

That is, in your unconscious state, you didn't think you were handing your problems to someone else for a solution. But you were doing that all the time. The only difference is that now you have them serve your real (conscious) purpose ~ that of winning the games you set up.

Interestingly, the fact is that people do have an endless list of their own problems. Some of them they'll never get to, in their entire lifetime. And I observe that they are always interested in taking on more. ~ so you might as well get yours solved, before they get to any of the others. If you will simply leave them with *recognition* for what they've done for you, they will actually appreciate you for what you've done for them. Now that's fair, isn't it?

Being "unreasonable" with others is only part of the secret to winning the big game; another clue is in being unreasonable with yourself ~ especially about where you want to go with your life. And the answer begins on the next page.

5. HOW TO GET WHERE YOU REALLY WANT TO GO IN LIFE

OR

"HOW TO MAKE EVERY DAY YOUR BIRTHDAY!"

You ask me: "What is your purpose in life? Where on Earth are you going?" My reply: "I can only know where I already am. So that's where I'm going."

Without question, the above makes absolute nonsense to you. Or, said another way, you can't relate your pictures on the videotape to it. And that equals a meaningless statement. (Only for the moment-come back and re-read it after you've finished this chapter.)

A discussion of your life's purposes has to begin with a discussion of a phenomenon I choose to call SPACE. Only this time it's *your* space. Let's go all the way back to the beginning now ~ to the time when you were a single cell, formed by the sperm from your father and the egg from your mother.

Look at that. See you when you were back there looking around, and the entire thing called 'you' was no bigger than a 'dink' on the head of a pin. A thousand of you could fit onto one dot on a piece of paper. It would take ten million of you to fill a thimble. Now imagine that you ended up at the bottom of the filled thimble. How easy it would have been to wipe you out back then. No effort at all. As a matter of fact, a simple sneeze could have blown you against a wall with enough force to do you in.

But then you wouldn't be here (and now!), big as all getout, reading these pages. So what got you here? Blind luck? Madam Fortune? Fate? Oh no, you don't get off that easy. YOU DID THAT TO YOU!

The truth is that *you* expanded your space from that single cell, out to the space that you occupy in the world right now. And you *do* occupy space. Get with the idea of the space you occupy in the world. Look at the fact that when you're in a place in the world, *nothing else can be*. Everything else moves out of the way. This is scientific fact: "No two things can occupy the same space at the same time."

And in order for you to begin to understand where you're going in life, you must first understand WHERE IT IS THAT YOU COME FROM. And the fact is that you come from your space. What I want to do at this point is to have you take the time necessary to take an in-depth look at your space. You call it your *body*.

What I would like you to do now is read through the following instructions once ~ twice if you feel the need ~ then put the book down and complete the exercise.

First, choose a place to sit down where it's comfortable for you, and close your eyes. Let your arms hang freely and relaxed; not crossed. Same with your legs. But don't lie down; I want you to stay conscious.

With your eyes closed, get the idea of relaxing your body and taking a look at what's going on in there. Look at the fact that your bones are the super-structure; and the skin is what holds it all in. Actually go down into your feet, and look around at what's going on there. Then move up into your ankles. And into your calves, knees, thighs, and then up into the area of your groin and buttocks. Just be there — look around and find out what's happening. Don't worry about the specific position of your organs ~just look carefully at whatever pictures come up for you. Move up through your diaphragm into your lung area and then look at your heart. Go up into your neck, then out into your arms, one at a time, and see what's there. Then go up into your head. Take a look behind your eyes, in the sinus area, and then look around your brain. Good.

Now get the idea of relaxing several key tension areas in your head. The first is the muscles between your eyes. Tighten them ~ then relax them. Just let them go. Now the jaw muscles. Grit your teeth, then let those muscles go. Relax them. Finally, your tongue! Let it lie on the floor of your mouth. Just relax.

If you have pains, aches, or are just plain tired, look at where those things are happening with you. Locate each of them. How far in? How far down? What color? Moving? Any thoughts about it? Considerations? Judgments? Do any videotape pictures come up about it?

Now I want you to re-read the instructions. Then, put the book down and follow them. Come back when you're finished. If it takes you half an hour or 45 minutes, that's ok, too. I'm not going anywhere (I'm already there, if you recall).

Great. I want you to really get into being conscious about your body space — because a lot of things happen there when you're unconscious that you won't let happen when you're totally conscious about things.

Like headaches. Next time you get one, go into your space, and take a long, hard look at it. Ask the above questions about it as you look. Maybe you won't get any results, I can never know what's going on with you. But go *through* the experience.

Next, I want you to get the idea that you already KNOW a

great deal about your space. (The fact is that you know all there is to know about it, but you needn't get hung up on that for the moment.) And when it comes to those things that you know about your space, you handle them naturally, and without any effort on your part at all. And you handle them perfectly. You *know* exactly, and intuitively, what to do with those portions of your space that you know about. Example: you know that you're a woman or a man. And nobody ever had to tell you how to handle that. (Oh, sure, people may have *thought* that you needed lessons, but that only makes them right. It doesn't make you need the lessons.) From your space, you look out at the world and see it. Nobody had to tell you how to do that either. In fact, there's no human being alive who could tell you *how* to do that. Same is true of hearing and smell and touch. You *knew* how to use them all along.

Now as you move away from those basics, you begin to think that someone *taught* you how to do the rest. For example, you may think that someone actually taught you how to walk. That's a lie. You did that to you. You simply expanded your space to include walking, and then you walked. People who were there just got to observe what was happening. They had no control over you whatsoever. If you don't accept that, fine. Go find someone who can't walk, and teach him to do it. But I want you to *explain* it to him. Tell him how to shift his weight and lift his feet, one at a time. And how to put the balancing act together. Could you write the "walking lessons" into a textbook and sell it? Why hasn't someone done that?

Because there's no way. When you take a hard look at walking, you will see that kids are on their own way to expanding their space to include it. You can only watch it. You can't speed it up; you can't slow it down. And you can't stop it either — because he knows where he's going. He's going to walk!

Are you ready for. this?

THE ONLY THINGS YOU CAN *EVER* DO IN LIFE ARE THOSE THINGS YOU EXPAND YOUR SPACE TO INCLUDE. AND THOSE THINGS COME FROM YOUR "NATURAL RIVER," OR YOUR "SOURCE". AND IF OTHER PEOPLE HADN'T GOTTEN IN THE WAY AND INTERFERED WITH YOU, YOU WOULD HAVE GONE WHERE YOUR SPACE EXPANSION

WAS (quite naturally) TAKING YOU. AND HAD A
HAPPY GRIN ON YOUR FACE — ALL THE TIME.

AND IF YOUR LIFE IS SCREWED UP NOW, IT'S
ONLY BECAUSE PEOPLE GOT IN YOUR WAY AND
STARTED SHOUTING "YOU CAN'T DO THAT!!"
AND THEN THEY PUT THINGS IN YOUR WAY TO
INSURE THAT YOU DIDN'T GET THERE. AND
THEN THEY STARTED GIVING YOU *INSTRUCTIONS*
ABOUT WHAT YOU SHOULD BE DOING WITH
YOUR LIFE.

And if you haven't got a certain smile on your face 95%
of the time ~ every day ~ you're a loser. Because you
believed them and made a decision (not a choice) to run
your life the way THEY said to run it.

And now you're screwed up. Because you're rowing
against your river. And you ain't going to win that one. All
you can do is TRY ~ for a lifetime.

That's admittedly a little difficult to accept. And since I
want you to really get it, let's keep going with the example
we started with: Kids. When you look you'll remember

that you were there once. Even though most of us act like we weren't.

Kids are absolutely beautiful. Uncluttered with all the "do's" and "don'ts" when they start out. Even you can see that. In fact, it's one of the rare events in the world that you see just like it is.

And the reason is that before their lives get tampered with, kids are riding their natural rivers. And they're happy as little larks doing it.

Now I want you to get the idea that kids know where they're going with their lives, if people would just create a safe space for them to explore, and then expand their space. They know what they need to know about them. And believe me, it would absolutely bowl you over to see what kids can do when they don't run into adults who instruct them that they "can't."

But, when kids hear, "You can't," or "You shouldn't" often enough, they begin to adopt their acts. That is, they begin to assume the values of the people who incessantly chant "rules" in their ears. So the acts start at a very early age. That is, kids are taught (instructed) that they should try to be actors.

Now when you look, you will see that nobody acts well. The people you call "good actors" aren't acting at all, they *are*. They have the ability to climb into the moccasins of the scripted role and live there. They ride that river. And that ain't acting, baby, it's life.

BECAUSE NO HUMAN BEING CAN "TRY" TO DO ANYTHING. You will either do it, or you won't.

What? A kid tries to walk? Another lie. He's either walking for a few steps or he's on his ass. And you can't try to swim. You're either swimming, or you're drowning. No in-betweens. Can you pick up a 400 pound weight? What you call TRYING is actually not picking it up.

You have a remarkable ability which you never acknowledged before. It is: TO LOOK AT A SITUATION AND *KNOW* WHETHER YOU CAN DO IT.

And I mean really *know* the answer for you. And all I'm saying is that if you can see that you can do it, go ahead and do it. You'll get the knack of it, because you know you can. And, if you look ahead and see that you can't, don't waste your time trying.

The problem with the world that fractures me is that people waste their lives trying. The trouble with the world is that it has told you by sticking you in a particular vise and clamping you in, that "THIS IS WHAT YOU WILL TRY TO DO WITH YOUR LIFE." AND YOU, YOU ASSHOLE, YOU'RE TRYING TO ACT THAT OUT.

And the world even has its "standard" formula for you — it's called the "HAVE" ~ "DO" ~ "BE" system.

The world starts out by telling you "Here are the acceptable things for you to aspire to. Pick one." So you do. (After all, you have no choice in the matter; only a decision.)

And then the games start: If you think you want to BE a ballerina, you must first HAVE all the gear ~ pointed shoes and a tu-tu. And you must also HAVE an instructor, and you must DO all the things she tells you to do. And if you try real hard, someday you might get to BE a ballerina.

If you think you want to BE an engineer, you must first

HAVE all the textbooks and a slide rule, then you must enroll in college and DO everything the professor tells you to do, and then, if you really try, you might get to BE an engineer.

The saddest commentary of all is that people who follow the system ~ and most do ~ end up rowing like hell against their natural river for a lifetime, trying to stay even, and then they go down being dead right about the way they ran their lives.

Now look at life, and understand that not one good (genuine) ballerina, accountant, engineer or whatever is made by the "HAVE ~ DO ~ BE" system. Not at all. You either are or you aren't. Or you end up trying.

Parents should simply provide a safe space for their kids to look and know who and what they are. Then let them "do," and then they'll quite naturally "have."

Schools should be CREATED WITH THE SOLE PURPOSE OF HAVING PEOPLE LOOK AT THEIR LIVES, FIND THEIR NATURAL RIVERS, AND CLIMB ABOARD THEIR INNERTUBES.

The only problem with the world's "HAVE ~ DO ~ BE" system is that it's *ass backwards*, that's all. You can only be what you already are. And you are many things. You can have an infinite number of games going at once, all of them constructed so that you're riding your natural river and end up winning them all. But you can't try to win any of them.

If you're in a rightness game now, your problem is that you're rowing so hard against the river you're in that you can't even entertain the notion of getting into another game. So you're stuck in the wrong game, and don't have the energy at the end of the day to look for a new one.

Now look at your life from the standpoint of what I've said: that you can only be what you already are. Because when you are, you will then do all the things those people do and will have everything they have. In that order. I'm sorry if you don't like it, because that's the way it is.

And before you jump to the conclusion that Norman Vincent Peale was right; "positive thinking" was the answer all along — STOP.

I said you look ahead, and you *know* that you can do it, or you can't.

Can you get up out of your chair and walk out the door? When you look at that, if you declare to yourself that, "I can," then at that point you have already DONE it. Your mind has checked that off as "ok," and you can start to entertain the notion of what it is you're going to do after you're out the door. The only thing between you and actually being out the door is SPACE AND TIME. You're out the door, and you will know ~ INTUITIVELY ~ if something ~ anything~ gets in your way. And then, when you're conscious about where you're going, you will have a choice about whether you want to be derailed by something that is in your way. If you're on your way out the door and you notice that the TV is on, you get to see very clearly that the program represents a "derail" to your purpose of getting out the door. Then you have the choice about whether to stop and watch the program, keep going, turn around, quit, whatever. And whatever it is that you choose, you're responsible for it.

Can you go to Las Vegas and *lose* $1,000 for me? Now if

you say to yourself, "You're a fool, but, to answer your question, yes, I can do that," then consider it done. The minute you look ahead and see what's so for you, you've already lost the $1,000. It's already gone. You can begin to plan what you'll do after you leave Caesar's Palace. The only thing between you and actually getting rid of the money is space and time. And, if I meet you in Pittsburgh and try to derail you to Portugal for a fun week in the sun, you know I'm getting in the way of your losing my $1,000. Then you have a choice: Vegas or Portugal? Or will you pull the Golden Gate diver act? Or what is it that you choose?

BUT CHOOSE YOU MUST.

Someone calls you on the phone and tells you that your youngster has fallen off his skateboard and his head is bleeding and you'd better get there. You look ahead and know you're there. And nothing gets in your way. You're already helping that kid. Period.

Now take the time necessary to look at your life. Look at the things you know you can do, and see that the actual process of doing them is *effortless*. Getting them done requires nothing but time and space. Put the book down, and take the time to run some pictures on your videotape playback machine. Come back when you've finished the exercise.

GET THIS: WHEN YOU LOOK AND *KNOW*, YOU'RE ALREADY THERE. WHEREVER "THERE" IS FOR YOU.

And Dr. Peale is off course. You can't grit your teeth, put on all the positive think plus signs, and try to get there. You're either there or you ain't.

And now I've got you: Question: Can you go to Las Vegas and *double* $1,000 for me? What? You say you'll try? Forget it. Look ahead and know what you're going to do. Don't try your act on me. I know when you're acting. Now what the hell is it that you're going to do?

What I'm getting at is not to punish you (which is equal to making you wrong). What I want you to look at and clearly see is whether or not you can go to Las Vegas and *double* $1,000 for me. Now if you look at that and say, "No, I can't," that's totally OK with me. You've saved me $1,000, and you've saved all that time you would have spent trying, and then felt guilty about when you ended up losing. Just be at truth with yourself, and quit trying to do things. You will only end up doing it or not doing it. Trying is something that happens on the way, and it doesn't relate at all to results. Or winning games. Look at trying, and, if it doesn't work for you, dump it from your act. Just forget it. Leave it behind you, there on the videotape. You're now oriented toward the present and the future so why choose to use it again?

LOOK AHEAD AND KNOW ~ AND THEN DO IT. OR, LOOK AHEAD AND KNOW ~ AND THEN DON'T GET INTO THAT GAME.

BUT DON'T TRY! BECAUSE THE TRUTH IS THAT YOU CAN'T TRY.

Take a look at your natural river. What are you? Stop playing games with yourself ~ play with others, to win. And I want you to admit the truth: that you can't try. Where's your river going? Are you riding with it? Or are you rowing against it?

Are you a carpenter?

Are you a businessman?

Are you a housewife?

Who and what are you?

Don't you see that there is no effort if you're riding with your river?

Here's a beautiful example for you: You wake up one morning, and are you ever sick. I mean, you've got a temperature by the thermometer, you up-chucked your breakfast, and you know you're just plain sick. And I acknowledge that. You are truly ill.

But, what I want to talk about is getting well. You've got a choice: Get well, or die with your sickness. Now if you choose to get well, your lifetime of adult instructions tells you to get to a doctor. Pronto. So you do. And now you're in his office.

Let's assume that he takes the point of view that there's nothing wrong with you. I mean, he's done all the tests, and looked at all your parts. Listened to you and what's going on with every talent that he has. And then he told you: "I can't find anything wrong with you. Go back to work."

Now, if you're unconscious, you immediately proceed to cancel his vote. You say he's incompetent, and dump him. And you call another doctor. "What's wrong with me? I've got to be right ~ dammit, I'm sick!" The fact is that you are both ~ you are, in fact, sick. And you are getting well. You know that. But you never looked at it that way. A doctor gets in the way only to observe that you are getting well, or that you are dying.

And the doctors in the world who know what's going on with human beings, know that there's nothing they can do to change the choice that you've already made. So the smart ones don't tell you that you're not sick (i.e., that you're wrong), they give you a placebo. Do you realize how many placebos are "prescribed" by the doctors of the world each year?

And the truthful doctors (who tell you they can't find anything) aren't financially successful. They don't get to make $375,000 every year and drive convertible Beamers. They only get to be wrong, and to lose unconscious patients in the process.

And the rightness doctors, who are stuck in the act of doctor, just agree with you, and prescribe something. So you think he earned his money. The visit to his office cost you $250, and the prescription cost you more. And, for all that money, you will end up being right. And you do.

In the few remaining pages of this chapter, I'm going to introduce you to two of the most fascinating, successful game players I've seen. They prove that knowing where you're going is all you need to get there.

First, meet my Uncle Don, who is an absolutely fantastic human being. Now as I look at him, what I see is that no one ever had the time to tell him that he couldn't do things. He was a depression kid. And at that time, the name of the game was real survival. How do we eat tomorrow? How do we keep a roof over our heads?

As a result, Don was on his own. And the things he can do would blow your mind. That man can get into anything and end up fixing it. I mean everything. He can take a look and tell you how to build a wood cabinet; make a pool table; play magician; wire a building; fix a TV, "soup up" a car; create a guitar from nothing but wires and strings; ad infinitum. There is literally nothing he can't do. And he knows that.

So one day I asked him: "What the hell is it with you that lets you get into anything on this earth and come out understanding it?" And his reply amazed me. He said, "I don't know. I just head into things to find out WHAT'S GOING ON in there, and in the end I find out what's going on."

Look at that. He never said, "I can't." He just headed into things with the knowledge that he was going to find out what was going on. And he found out. Always. The last time I saw him, he was ready to tear down a broken microwave oven (which he had never seen before) to find out what was going on in there. And I know that he found out what was going on in that oven. It's fixed. It works.

Now get ready for a blow-out: If I were in a car accident and ended up on the side of the road in a life-or- death situation where an operation was immediately necessary, I would want my Uncle Don to accompany any "doctor" in the world who could be brought to my 'rescue." And the reason is that he already knows that he's going to go in and find out "what's going on with me." Just like he tears down a clock, or a microwave oven.

By contrast, most doctors of the world are "practicing," because that's what their certificate says. They practice. Now you can trust your life to someone who's practicing. I want to be with someone who knows — and who's going to find out what's going on with me and fix it.

My Uncle Don never went beyond the sixth grade. He doesn't know what the hell's going on with the New York Stock Exchange. He doesn't know what Harvard stands for, let alone where it is. He just finds out what's going on with things, that's all. And then he fixes the problem.

And most of the doctors in the world followed the "HAVE ~ DO ~ BE" system. They aren't really doctors. They just acted out all the instructions that their parents/teachers/the world told them to act out. And they're still stuck in their acts. As I said before, they're "practicing." By their own admission. It's even printed on their wall boards. Look at that the next time you go into a doctor's office. Take a hard look at your doctor.

Understand that when one is making $300,000 or $400,000 per year in a "practice," it soon becomes ok to practice. No shit, if that isn't ok, what is? The financially successful doctors of the world see very early on that they are nothing more (and nothing less) than the guy who happens to get in the way of you going where you're going. Ninety-five percent of the time they see people, they can't really "fix" anything anyway.

Then they come to realize that the greatest part of their day consists of a WORD GAME, followed by the "prescriptions" they write. Get the notion that 95% of the words they write are nothing more than what you want to hear.

If you want to get to someone who can really get into you and find out what's going on with your system, go to my Uncle Don or to a doctor who knows what's going on with you. He's flowing with his natural river. He'll fix it. He's going to go in and find out what's wrong with you. No doubt about it.

And if you choose to play with a "practitioner," who will undoubtedly agree with you, you can go to a doctor who's rowing against his river. Or you can create a good doctor. You'll know a good doctor when you see him. For openers he won't lie to you — and won't take any B.S. from you, either.

One final point: when you get sick, get the idea that the first person to ask about it is you. Why did you do that to you? What's going on with you? Look and know if you need a doctor. Experience what happens the next time you look at a headache, or a cold, or a pain.

The point I want you to get from these examples is simply this:

YOU'RE ALREADY ON YOUR WAY SOMEWHERE. No, I can never know where that is, because you aren't me. But YOU can know. YOU <u>DO</u> KNOW— YOU JUST NEVER ADMIT IT TO YOURSELF. AND ACCEPT IT.

AND TAKE RESPONSIBILITY FOR IT.

And when you're on your way somewhere ~ it literally doesn't matter where it is ~ that's the only place you can get. (To be sure, someone can get in your way and derail you, but only if you're unconscious.) When you're conscious, you haven't been derailed. You've CHOSEN to go that way, and you're responsible for those actions. When you're derailed, someone else did it to you. The derailer did it to you, you derailee.

Let me share another example with you to validate what I've said about knowing where you're going: Meet my old boss, Irving The Millionaire. This guy came to Los Angeles in 1960 with nothing. The stories have it that he had less than $2,000 when he got there, but assume that the number was off by 5 times, and that he had $10,000. Even that can't make a two-bit hustler into what old Irving already was. A millionaire about 15 times over. Now he didn't know anybody, or anything about Los Angeles. And he had been exposed to such "glamour" industries as selling distressed ethnic records; importing bongo drums, buying broken gift shop wooden horses, gluing them and sanding "Los Angeles" off, then painting "Phoenix" on ~ and driving to the desert to sell two cases. He even made a bid on a ship that went down off the Palos Verdes Peninsula. Now that ship's still stuck in the water. But old

Irv, the boy from Brooklyn ~ he refused to get stuck in that act. He just kept choosing freely ~ because he was already a millionaire. And what he was, he is. Because that's where he was going, with no effort at all. He didn't "try" ~ he was already there!

Now, I want you to look very carefully and really get just this one notion: Neither my Uncle Don nor Irving The Millionaire ever followed the world's "HAVE ~ DO ~ BE" system. They never really heard the world when it said they shouldn't or couldn't do things. They never had the time to stop and try to accumulate all the things the supposed "experts" had to have to enter their chosen game in life.

Get the idea that "Keeping up with the Joneses" is just that. Trying to row like hell to stay even. And it doesn't work.

Take Irving. I personally met a number of people who knew him "back when" he didn't have two cents in his pocket, couldn't pay the rent, and had a list of creditors as long as his arm. Believe me when I tell you that each of them knew that his train was going to roll into millionaire's station ~ even though he couldn't have liquidated all he had then for $5,000. And even now they recall that he didn't make many of them wrong as he rolled onward and upward. The business community remembered him; waitresses remembered him; his employees remembered him. Old Irving was going where he was going, so why upset people along the way? He got the cheese!

Take Uncle Don. He never had the money to go out and buy all the tools one "needs" to fix things. He worked in the beginning with what he knew and one screwdriver. Over time, of course, he got all the things the "experts" are supposed to have, but the point is that he didn't follow the "HAVE ~ DO ~ BE" system. He did it backwards. He was ~ then he did ~ then he got. And he didn't try at all. He didn't have to. He was already there.How do you compare with Uncle Don and Irving The Millionaire? Take a careful look at your life and know if you're trying; if the very process of living every day is an "effort." If it is, you're not going to get there from where you are. "Trying" is what makes those "statistics" we see every day about the incredible number of people who are not satisfied with their work; their lovers; their friends; their mates; their whatevers. They keep trying to stay even; to row against their natural rivers.

Let's take a moment to tie a number of phenomena together, and look at the mechanism of what's going on. Remember the function of your mind ~ the only reason it exists: to keep you right; to make you survive; and to do that it serves up those pictures from the past which it thinks relate to your survival in that situation. And then recall that I said you can only be what you already are.

Fine. Now let's move into a situation and examine it. You're sitting in an important meeting, or in a classroom, and discover that you're sleepy. But it would be wrong for you to go to sleep there, so you can't do that, and you end up being frustrated. What happened? Simple: your mind served up the pictures of frustration as the survival mechanism. That makes it ok for you to be sleepy.

Now, that was when you were unconscious. When you're conscious about your life, what'll happen is this: You notice that you're sleepy, acknowledge it, accept it, and take responsibility for choosing to be sleepy. And you look ahead and know that you will get some sleep. You are already asleep. Next you have a conscious choice to make: to sleep now, or to delay. You'll find a number of things happening with you when you get to the place I've just described — first, you'll notice that it's totally alright for you to have chosen to be sleepy. And the reason that it's totally alright is that it's there ~ it's unchangeable. It's in the past. And second, because you look ahead and know that you will, in fact, get some sleep, it's totally ok for you to *choose* not to sleep now. It's amazing how awake you can be when you *choose* not to sleep. And the most important thing to note is that you get to skip the frustration. You cut off your mind from serving it up because you know that frustration doesn't serve your purpose, and it doesn't make you survive either.

There's another very important point to be aware of: the fact that you are at source; that is, you created the sleepiness. No one did that to you. No thing did it to you. Now, when you were unconscious, you thought you sort of "discovered" those things that were going on with you. Not so. You created them. And you're responsible for them. Look at mornings when you wake up. You always thought that you "found out" how much energy you have each day. No way, baby. You're the source of your energy, or lack of it. You chose to have an abundance of it ~ or none. And you're responsible for what you chose. And when you reach the condition in life of having that fact be ok with you ~ no matter what you chose ~ you'll find that it's easy as hell, and effortless, to deal with it.

The same is true of other events you bring into your life. Look at those times when you got up late for work. The alarm didn't go off. So you blamed the clock, or your wife. The truth is that you chose not to wake up. You're responsible for that. Because you can choose to wake up when you want to. To the exact minute. But you know that. So why do you play games with yourself? What do you get out of trying? Why do you lie about it?

There's a good phrase to summarize one of the key points in this chapter. It is that you can't have what you have to have.

Take money (a very popular subject). If you've made a decision that you have to have a lot of money in order to survive, you're not going to get there. If you're gritting your teeth every day, trying to do all the things necessary to get a lot of money, you're playing a game with yourself that you're not going to win. The place you have to get to is acceptance of the fact that you haven't got a lot of money, and that you're responsible for the lack of it. Next, it has to be totally ok with you because it's in the past. Then (and only then) do you get a choice in the matter: do you choose to have money in the future? If you do, you'll get there, without trying.

That is, if you look ahead and know that you're there, the process of actually getting there is effortless. And the only things between you and getting there are space and time. Oh, sure, you'll have choices to make on the way — lots of them. And you'll undoubtedly make some mistakes as you progress. But when you're fully responsible for those mistakes, you clean them up — fast. You're never stuck in the losing game of trying to edit the videotape. You're looking ahead, having learned from the experience of watching carefully as the shots were made, and always having the opportunity to go back and just stand by and look. And you've given up being right in the process.

In contrast, if you look ahead and know that you can't do something, or that you aren't something, but then you decide that (for whatever reasons) you really should try to do it/be it/"get there," you're putting on an act and rowing against your river. And when you're trying, you aren't going to get there. If you have an enormous amount of stamina and staying power, you might be able to stay even, or even manage to make some headway. But the minute you relax slightly and begin to look at your life, you also begin to lose ground.

The final point I want to communicate on this is the truth about an old piece of folklore that I used to encounter "way back when" that still holds some real meaning for me: It's the notion that you get to do "what you want to do" on your birthday. Remember that one? Now when I look and see myself back there, dumping my act on my birthday, it has real meaning for me. As a kid, I can remember doing exactly what I wanted to on my birthday. And it was really an exhilarating feeling. Easy to do. A good day. Well, you can go through the experience of validating what I'm telling you about your life ~ and every day will be your birthday.

By now you're probably wondering: How can I know when I'm really there versus making a decision? How do I know where my river's truly heading?

Try turning the page. (Notice that I said "try," and that I did not say "turn the page.")

When you're tired of trying, go ahead and turn the page.

6. A PLAYFUL EXERCISE ON YOUR RIVER

Well, it sure is nice to be here with you, as you stand ready to take a look at your river, and where it's going. When you get to see it clearly, I'll guarantee you that your inner smile will be so wide that even that super scooter stuntman, Evel Kneivel, couldn't jump across it.

Because when you know something, it's totally different than believing it, thinking it, or rationalizing it. You just know it's the truth, that's all.

Now I want you to start this exercise by repeating the one we did earlier. That is, to choose a chair, sit down, open your body, uncross your hands and legs, close your eyes, and look around in your space. Start with your feet and continue on throughout your body, then complete the exercise by relaxing the tenseness between your eyes, your jaw muscles, and finally your tongue. Just let your body relax.

Now put the book down, and complete the exercise. Come back when you've finished. Take as long as you take.

Great. The truth is that you can accomplish a lot by taking five minutes in the morning and again in the evening to go into your space and just look around. Because you are a physical being. And that means that everything you feel or experience has to start somewhere in your space. Including thoughts. They don't get "handed" to you by some outside source. On the contrary: Everything that you experience starts somewhere in your space. Nowhere else. With no one else. You're the center.

That brings us to the point of beginning to look ahead at where your river's flowing: toward your real purposes in life. First, you should look and know that those purposes can only deal with three things: PEOPLE, PLACES, AND THINGS. That's all, because that's all there is in real life.

So our purpose in this exercise is for you to begin to get the notion of what (people, places and things) your river includes. Because that's where you're going. And that's who and what will be there.

To begin the exercise, I want you to get the idea of being in your space. Then go into your space, and once again look around. See what's going on. Get the idea of clearing it. Rinsing away all the debris you've been carrying around all this time.

Great. Now get the idea that your space is made of clear glass. That is, your body is a glass container. And I want you to go down in your space, and look out. Go down into your feet, and look out from there. Up through your ankles, calves, thighs, and look out. Look out from your back. See what it must be like for people who are following you. Go out into your arms, and look out from there. Then go up into your head; look out from your eyes. Go up into your hair follicles, and look out from there.

Fine. Now get the idea that your glass container is going to fill up with a warm, orange-colored liquid. And it's going to start to fill up at your feet. Just kind of flow in and fill the glass container. You can see your feet filling up first, then your ankles, and your calves, with the warm orange liquid. When it gets to your arms, it'll run down quickly all the way out to the tips of your fingers. Then it'll fill up your arms and move up into your neck. And then on up into your head, filling the sinus cavities, then your brain area, and all the way up to the hair follicles at the top of your head.

Good. Now get the idea that you're going to go down into your space again, and look at the warm liquid, and at your space. You get to play "diver." So dive down and look around. Swim right up to the glass, and peer out.

All right. Now get the idea that you have two sets of "valves" ~ one at the tips of your big toes and one at your fingertips. Then go down and release the valves on your toes — but just enough so that the liquid begins to drain out slowly from the ends of your toes.

Fantastic. Now look at your head; see the liquid moving away from your hair follicles, leaving your brain area.

Get the idea that the liquid is cleaning your space ~ and

that you've never had an internal washing before. When the liquid drains out, it's taking all the debris and lies, all the sublimated "junk" you've been carrying around for most of your life. Great. Notice that your brain has a few drops of liquid left on it; just like a car after it's been through an automatic wash. So, shake your head gently and get those drops off.

Get the feeling of relief from the weight of the liquid that's leaving your space. It was terribly difficult to lift your legs when they were full; as the liquid drains away, realize how easy it is.

Good. When the liquid has drained away from your legs, recall that you haven't yet released the valves in your fingers; your arms are still full. So go ahead and open those valves and watch the liquid drain from your arms.

OK. Now go back in and look at your space again. Notice how clean it is. Like it's never been before. In fact, you never even bothered to notice what was going on in your space. Look it over again. See what's happening with you now that you've cleaned it. Kind of glows all over, doesn't it? Breathe deeply. Notice how easy that becomes.

Great. Now get the notion that you're going to transport your space ~ and look around the world. And what you're going to be looking for is that place where you'd really be happy. Whether on a seashore, or on a mountain, or in a tall, green pine forest, or wherever. Just take whatever comes up. And when you find that you're really happy there, smile with yourself. Because it was YOU who found it.

Now take a moment and just look around. No one's there. And it's your place in the sun. Take the time necessary to explore what's there. Get a feel for the sounds of the place. The animals. The water. The trees. The grass. The sky. It's really good to be there, isn't it? Not a care in the world. Breezes blowing. And life's great.

Fantastic. Now I want you to get the idea that you're going to build a little workshop, right there. Your center. A place where you can always come to work, practice, review, study, build, listen, or just take a long look at things. All yours. And you can always relax there. Kick back and take it easy, whenever you choose to do that. All by yourself ~ with everything left behind.

OK. We're ready now to start building your center. First, get the notion of what it'll be like. We want to make it just one big, expansive room. As big as you like. But one room, where lots of things can take place.

What will it be made of? Wood? Cement? Bricks? When you get the idea, bring that material in, and join in with the workmen who are building your center. Help carry the materials. Do some work on it. Install a window, if you ordered windows. Put on a door. Are there locks? Make sure they work.

Good. Now go inside and look outside. Get the feeling that you're really going to fall in love with the place when it's finished. Look out the windows at what's going on outside. Try the doors, and see how easily they swing open and closed.

Now get the idea of the finish on the walls inside. When you get the material selected, bring it in, and once again help to build it. Or do it all yourself. Do you want workmen to assist you? It's your choice. Go about finishing the walls. Stand back again and really enjoy the feeling of pride you have now that your own workshop center has come this far.

Alright. Now let's think about the floors. What are you going to use to construct them? How will you finish them? Will you lay carpeting? Hardwood? Choose a floor to your liking, and what's going to cover it, and see the materials being brought in to make it all come together. Again, go out and help the deliverymen bring everything in. Tell them about what's going on there. Let them look around. Let them see the smile on your face.

Great feeling, isn't it?

OK, now put the floor in. See what you can do as a worker on your floor. When it's finished, just sit your body down on the floor and relax. Enjoy it. Know that it's yours. And that others come there only at your invitation.

Good. Now I want you to get up from the floor and walk around and review the whole thing. Look at the walls, and the ceiling, and out the windows, and at the floor, and really experience the good feelings you get — just being there.

Great. Now get the idea of bringing in your desk. First, think about your desk ~ and what it'll be like. Will it be wooden? Fiberglass? Leather-top? Old and with a rolltop? Modern? Expansive, so that it surrounds you? When you get the idea of your desk, bring in the materials and build it. Or, order it and see it being brought into your center.

OK. Now get the idea of your chair. I mean the chair that you want in your center. All right, now build it, or buy it, and bring it into your center.

Good. Sit down, lean back and look around at how perfect things really are. And there you are, right where you want to be, sitting back in your place in the world. Look out the windows. Notice how friendly everything is, because you built it.

Fine. Now get the idea that you're going to want a telephone in your center. On your desk. So, bring it in and see it installed. Now on this phone you can call anyone in the world, toll-free. You just dial, or push the buttons, or maybe you just call the operator, and tell her who it is that you want.

OK, now make sure the phone works. Pick it up, get the idea of who it is that you're going to call, and get that person on the line. Whoever answers, say hello to them. Ask what's been going on with their lives. Tell them that you're calling from your center, just to test the phone you had installed. Perhaps you'll want to tell them something that's been on your mind for some time. Ask if there's something he's wanted to tell you, but never has. Just chat and be there with that person for awhile. Great. Now tell the person that you have to be going — but that you will call again. And then say goodbye, after thanking the person for spending valuable time with you.

Now we're on our way to adding another feature to your center. In the left-hand drawer of your desk there's a file where all the facts in the world are stored. All you have to do is thumb through the alphabetical index, find the situation that you want to look at, open the file, and it's there. Great. Flip through the file for an event. Find it alphabetically, pull it out, and look at the history of what happened then. What year was it? Who was there? What was going on? Was it a cold or warm day? What were they saying? Great. Now close the file and put it back in its place. It'll always be there for you to refer to, somewhat like Google.

Next, I want you to open the right-hand drawer and notice that there are files containing all the people in the world. Each person has his or her own file, and again all you have to do is flip through alphabetically and select whoever you want. Choose a file, and put it on your desk top, and see who's in the file you chose. Look at the pictures of that person when he was very young. See where he lived. Look at his parents. What year was it then? Where did that person go to school? Look at his high school days. What was going on with him? What was being said?

Fine. Now close the file and replace it in its proper position. Close the drawer and know that you can always open it and that everyone in the world is in there, if you want or need to refer to them.

Great. Now, as you sit at your desk, I want you to get the notion of installing a big digital clock on the wall of your center. This clock will have one amazing performance feature: it can be turned backwards or forwards to any hour, day, or year, and you have control of where it's set.

And right next to the digital clock is a videotape playback machine, which will rack up the pictures of that time, and play them just for you. Next, turn the controls of the digital clock back 15 years, exactly to the hour, day, and place. Now run the videotape machine and look at what was going on with you that day. See who was there. Listen to what was being said. Just stand back and watch it. What were the people wearing? Was it warm or cold? How did you feel? Any considerations you have of that day? Any decisions you made that day which you recall?

Fine. Now turn the dials of the clock back to the present, and know that you can always use the clock and the video machine to replay anything that's happened in your life, and also to look forward to see what might be going on.

Alright. Now we want to construct a stage in your center. Get the idea that it'll be elevated somewhat, so that you will be in the "audience" when you're sitting at your desk and must look up at about a 15 degree angle to watch what's going on. Now build the stage, complete with a curtain, microphones, floodlights, and whatever else you choose to install there. Next, come back down to your chair, relax, and get the idea of testing the stage to see that it works exactly as you planned it.

So, turn on the floodlights, and the sound system, and get the idea that someone you know is standing behind the curtain, waiting to be introduced. OK. Now open the curtain and see who that is. Stand up and greet him warmly. Welcome him to your center. Tell him that it's great to see him . . . and that you created all that he sees. Ask him what's been going on with him. Tell him what's been going on with you. Is there anything you've wanted to tell him, but haven't? Tell him now, and experience his reaction. Know that it's a great feeling to be in the security of your center, and let him see that you're quite at ease with yourself, and that you're really enjoying having him there with you. Fine. Now thank the person for visiting you, and tell him that he's always welcome. Then say goodbye, close the curtain and shut off the lights and the microphones.

Fantastic. There's one more thing we want to install in your center. It's called an "Ability Cabinet." The first thing to do is to get the idea of constructing a cabinet that will contain the clothes of each ability ~ all the costumes and equipment certain "able" people have. It'll have to be airtight and have a place to hang things and to store things. Now bring in all the materials and construct it. When you're finished, admire the workmanship, and put it against a wall in your center, then get the idea of hanging two ability suits in there. Choose two things you've always wanted to do, but never quite got 'round to doing. See the things that those people have ~ and select and create all those things for you. They'll be custom-made, of course, and the best available in the world. Put on the uniform, and get the idea of how comfortable it is when things really fit you. Move around with the uniform on. Get the notion of doing a practice session of about two minutes duration with all the equipment that you need, just like a pro.

See yourself there ~ and how easy it is to "get" what you're supposed to get. Since it'll be only two minutes long, know that you're not even going to have the time to get tired. Then just breeze through your practice session. Fine. Now come back into your center, undress, and hang the ability suit back in your cabinet. Stand back and know that you can put the suits for any ability in there, then bring them out and wear them, whenever you choose. Great. Now close the door to your cabinet, return to your desk and relax.

Fantastic! Here you are in your center, with all those things to do! Let's inventory them: First, there's the place in the world where you've chosen to build your center. Look around there ~ and see that it's really great. Then look over your center itself ~ from the outside. Walk around it. Touch the walls. Know that it's yours. OK. Now go inside and let the knowledge that you built your center overwhelm you all at once. Isn't it unbelievable? You built it exactly as you wanted it. And there it is! The floor. Your desk. Your chair. The phone. The files on the world and the other file on all the people. The telephone you installed and the fact that you can call anyone on it. ~ anytime you choose.

Great feeling, isn't it?

Now get the idea of reviewing the other things in your center. Look at the clock, which you can set for anytime you choose, then have it run the pictures of what was or will be happening.

And your stage. With all that fantastic equipment. The curtain. The floodlights and the sound system. Where you can have the world come in and perform for you. Or have someone in just to chat. Or meet new people. Or whatever you choose.

And then there's your Ability Cabinet. Where you can create the things the "experts" have, and store them there for your personal use. And you can take out those custom-made things, wear them, and practice until you "get it." And you can store in that cabinet whatever abilities you choose to store there.

Now I want you to get the feeling of self-satisfaction. And I want you to know that it comes from you ~ because it's your center. You built it, I didn't. You have the keys to it. You can come there, dump all your acts, and just lie down and relax on the floor. For as long as you want. And you can go there to create, build, study, review, work, play, think; everything in the world that's "do-able," you can do there. Whatever you choose. And you can invite anyone in the world to come there. And not feel threatened by anything. And be at ease with all those that you invite to visit. You're the host. And that's your center. And your life.

Now you've just begun to see what your river consists of. And where it's going. And where you're going. Get the idea that you can go to your center anytime you choose. Go there and look at your life. Know when you're happy. Know where you're going with your life.

Understand that you can bring anything into your center, work with it, or just look it over. Review it. Or just let it be there. Study it, or ignore it. Keep it there or remove it. You're the only one who says what comes and goes.

And when you become conscious about your center, and who you choose to invite there, and the things you choose to have there, and the place that the center is, you'll find that you begin to live there. And it's magnificient! Now, when you're in the middle of the hustle and bustle of an experience, you'll just wander out to your center and create something. And relax.

BECAUSE THAT'S WHERE YOU'RE GOING. Literally. And most definitely. The thing that's incredible about what I've told you is that it's not a fairy tale. When you're living in your center, that's where you're going. And the people you tell about it will do nothing but help you get there faster. And it'll all be effortless. And no one will be wrong for letting you win that game.

THE THING THAT WILL ABSOLUTELY ASTOUND YOU IS THAT WHEN YOU BEGIN TO BE CONSCIOUS ABOUT YOUR CENTER, IT WILL BEGIN TO COME TRUE. AND THEN, WHEN YOU COMMUNICATE ABOUT IT, IT *WILL* COME TRUE.

And you will know that you're responsible for it. Totally. Just like you were responsible for running your life on a "right/wrong" scale before.

And that's what I want you to look for: HARD FACT. Experience. Never let me or anyone else tell you that "things will be better" tomorrow. That if you just "keep trying," you'll get there someday ~ by magic. Oh, no~ you now know that you must validate things day by day and look at the world in the hard light called TRUTH. If you have no hard facts to demonstrate that your center is becoming a reality, then dump the act you've assumed.

Don't kid yourself ~ you've done that too long.

There's one additional point I want to make with you — it has to do with experiencing *events versus concepts*. Now the truth is that you can't experience a concept. You can only experience an event. Concepts are something you can't deal with ~ you can't clear up the pictures of a concept, because there aren't any. Concepts get you stuck in a losing game with yourself.

An example of a concept is, "My father and I don't get along." Or, "My life doesn't work." Still another is, "She doesn't understand me." Those kinds of statements are all bullshit.

It's events ~ specifics ~ that you can deal with; that you must deal with, if you want to cut off the pictures and be free to choose. The event is that "you had an argument with your father last Sunday afternoon about subject X." That's an event. You can clear that up. Similarly, your life isn't working because of events ~ specific games you set up and lost. Look at them. "I set up a game to go to a movie last Saturday night and didn't get there. Why did I do that to me?" When you get at the pictures of the event, it'll clear up. Then you can move on.

GET THIS: YOU CAN ONLY EXPERIENCE AN EVENT. YOU CAN NEVER EXPERIENCE A CONCEPT. JUNK YOUR CONCEPTS.

And just so we're totally clear — there's no "magic" in this book. That is, nothing's going to "happen" to you as a result of reading it. If your life gets better, it will be because you experience it. Or it won't happen. You see, like I told you, you can't experience a concept. And the words printed here are concepts. You must go through the experiences.

And when you really get at the specifics about your center ~ the place it's located, the people you invite there, the things you want there ~ it'll all be there. And you'll stand back in amazement and be awed by the power you've used in getting there. YOUR POWER. YOU DID IT TO YOU. You'll have the biggest grin on your face, and everyone invited there will be just as happy.

Time to get rid of all your acts — and get on with what life is all about — winning the game. And that consists of whatever you create. Nothing more ~ nothing less.

* * * * * * * * * * * * * * *

Now I suggest that you read this chapter into a recording device, and then play it back. Go into your space and follow your own instructions: build your center with your eyes closed. At the very least, re-read it very consciously before you move onto a discussion of how you get to be a leader and a problem-giver in the big game.

7. HOW GURUS GET MADE

OR

"WILL YOU AGREE WITH ME?"

This will be a fun chapter, because some amazing truths will emerge.

And to be certain that we're communicating, I will first provide you with my definition of a guru: it's simply a person who gets others to listen to him. When he talks, people pay attention.

So that lets out the guy who makes a declaration to himself that requires no "people involvement." Or, you get to sit at home and chant to yourself — "I am the king of the winter hearthfires." And the burning logs in front of you (naturally) say nothing. If you call that being the guru of hearthfires, I accept that. But I suggest that you always keep a sharp eye behind you at what/who is following. You might get burned. Similarly, I would suggest that you think twice before declaring to people that you are some other thing/character with dubious validation characteristics. Like Napoleon revisited. Because you already know that people can go fishing in their videotapes, and replay that action ~ even though they weren't there to experience it. And that means you're just as likely to end up being called an inmate as a guru. People can easily cancel your vote in the game ~ and make it stick.

Now you can begin to see quite transparently that the entire game of life is one of AGREEMENT. If other people don't agree with you, you're in big trouble. Think about that. How would you react if suddenly all your friends didn't listen to a thing you said? What would your reaction be if you kept yelling to the driver~ "Watch out — a red light!"~ but he ignored you and went sailing through? And the others in the car agreed with him that the light was green? How far would you get in your work if nobody agreed that what you were doing had value? How many copies of this book would sell if no one agreed that it was worth reading?

NOW! GET THE IDEA THAT NOTHING IN THE WORLD EXISTS, UNLESS THERE IS AGREEMENT BETWEEN/AMONG PEOPLE THAT IT DOES EXIST.

And that gurus are nothing more than people who make declarations (which require a picture reshuffling), and who get other people to agree with them.

Let's deal with the basics first: the agreement.

Who the hell says that David Letterman should get $10 million a year for telling us bedtime stories?

Who says that a man named Sassoon is worth $250 to clip your locks?

Who says that Helena Rubenstein gets more for her face mud than Elaine Bernstein of Boise, Idaho?

On and on, infinitely. Who puts VALUE in the game?

People do. You do. You're responsible for that. Or those things and those people wouldn't be there. Period.

Value is nothing but agreement. Who says that gold (as opposed to tin, for example) gets credited with value in the world? You do.

Now, you may choose to cast your vote vicariously, through someone called a "critic." But at the base of it all, you are still buying that critic's vote on the issue. Or the critic wouldn't be the critic. And that's all that value is.

How much value does a million U.S. greenbacks have if the people of Fishermans Island won't take them? "Sorry, sir, on this island we all agree that fisheyes are the tool for trading. You haven't got any, and waving all that paper makes about as much sense as taking a header off the Golden Gate bridge. You lose."

Want a classic example? Not long ago I went to a large metropolitan museum of "art." The reason I put that word in quotes is that it requires agreement. That is, no museum can exist for long if people don't agree that what they have inside represents "art." And that's the point of the example. While there, I saw a "hopper" (you know what that is, don't you?) cut in half and somehow affixed to a painted piece of plywood. Price tag: $22,500. Laugh if you will, but understand that if some other person agrees that it's worth $22,500, then that game was won by the hopper cutter/mounter. And he won it only because he got someone to agree that what he had created, in fact, was 'art.'

Now get the idea that no matter what game it is that you create, to the degree that it involves other people, you must get agreement if you expect to win it. And you already know one of the key elements of getting that agreement: just give up being right about it. Go out and win the games you set up, get all the cheese, give people recognition for serving your purpose, and keep going higher.

Now we're beginning to shed some light on what a guru does. Simple: Gurus do nothing but HAND OUT THE PROBLEMS, AND GET PEOPLE TO AGREE TO SOLVE THEM.

So elementary it borders on absurdity. A guru is the guy (or gal) who does a picture reshuffling, gets people to agree that the game he set up is worth playing, and then they begin to play his game. He's the source, however, and that is extremely important. Because the source gets to do one more thing: MAKE THE RULES.

Take a hard, cold look at that. Look at the gurus of the world, and see what's going on. Let's revisit one guru from the olden days: Alexander Graham Bell. Picture reshuffle: "We all talk to one another, so why not use this thing I've got here called a telephone?"

The first (and only necessary) step was for people to agree that his phone game was worth playing. After that, they set up this elaborate system, called a phone network. And people agreed to play it to the hilt; laying cables all over the world. It's so complex now that there must be two million people out there solving the problems that Bell created. And then came the mobile phone.

Look at Edwin Land, the guru who brought you the Polaroid camera game. He did a literal reshuffling of your pictures: "Wouldn't you like to skip the time it takes to process that film, and see it as fast as you shoot it?" Again (as always) the first step was to get agreement. They asked him how they could play that game. And now he's got all the cheese.

At this point, you're probably saying to yourself: "Alright. Sure, those guys got to be gurus. But they were idea men ~ they invented something. I'm not that creative."

Fine. I accept that. But I want you to look carefully at a question: Are you certain that Bell and Land and all of the "inventors" in the world were really the inventors, or just the guys who came up with the problem? I don't have the answer to that, but I want you to hang out with the question, because it's central to the issue.

And before you decide that you couldn't get other people to agree to solve your problems, have you looked carefully at that? Do you have ideas? How do you know that yours aren't as agreeable for solution as the next guy's? Have you ever thought about things that could get agreement in the marketplace of life?

Because I'm here to tell you flat out that in order for you to become a guru, you don't have to have anything but the problem identified. And you must get the agreement of other people that they should help you to solve it. You don't have to have the ability to build, or assemble, or even write the blueprints for ANYTHING. Once people agree with you, you're the guru, and then you get to do two things: MAKE THE RULES, AND KEEP HANDING OUT THE PROBLEMS.

Want additional proof? Let me share a specific experience with you that really makes my point come alive: for ten years after graduate school, I worked closely with the "gurus" of some of the largest companies in the United States. Two of them were billion-dollar giants in annual sales; another was in the $750 million category. By cold and analytical observation of those pictures of the past, I see now that the presidents of those New York Stock Exchange companies didn't really know any more than I did. But what I want you to get is that they were the gurus because I agreed that they were. And it didn't matter what they knew. All they did was to make the rules and hand out the problems for me (and the other employees) to solve. That's ALL there is to being a guru.

What makes you worth whatever compensation you

receive each year? I submit that it's agreement, and nothing more. If you told your company that you were worth $2 million next year, and they agreed, then what are you worth next year?

And nothing has to be logical about it. I know a guy in one of the companies I was in who got agreement from the president and board of directors that they should pay him $100,000 per year for twenty years to stay out of their class of business. All he did was agree not to compete with them for 20 years. Incredible, but true, in life's game of agreement. And there's no way for you to escape it. You gotta play, as long as you're around.

Stop now and take a careful look at the words printed above. Let them sink in. Be certain of where you are about gurus, and what makes them. Don't move on until you really get it.

Good. Here are a couple of additional examples to bring it even closer to home.

I listen to workers every day who say things like, "Ah, my boss doesn't know anything. I know ten times as much as he does." And I want to acknowledge that many (if not all) of them are correct. But the boss got them to agree that he's the boss and they're the workers. And it truly doesn't matter what he knows. He's still the boss. And at the base of it all, he's at least a semi-guru. Because he gets to hand out the problems. And the head guru of the business gets to do nothing but hand out problems and set the rules.

Moving right along — look at all the family-owned businesses in the world. And at all the workers therein who sit around and bitch when the "old man" makes his kid the president, and the kid "has never even set foot in the company." Fine, you go on and bitch about that, if you get something out of complaining. But the kid still remains the guru, because those people stay and agree that he is. They're still there solving his problems for him.

Get that: if they're still there solving his problems, he's still the guru. And if they didn't agree that he was the guru, they'd leave that game and create a new one. (I'll be the first to admit that it wouldn't be very reasonable for them to leave, but if they did, the kid would be left as the lonely guru of the winter hearthfire.) And the truth is that people do have the choice of staying or leaving each and every game they have going.

It's the same with our government. You're responsible for 9/11, Afghanistan, Iraq, and that whole convoluted mess down there in Washington, including the angry military/industrial quango perched like a mean bald eagle (now armed with drones instead of arrows) on top of the Pentagon. The world's current tragedy is defined by a comedy of error-heads, playing "survival of the fittest" mind games. And the generals are the gurus.

Now I know that you'd like to duck the responsibility for a lot of events by throwing them off to your diminutive stature in the world — "What can I do?" — but that doesn't let you escape the responsibility. Look at the opposite side of the coin: If you're not ultimately responsible, who the hell is?

The truth is that you put the gurus in place, by agreeing that they had a game worth playing.

And you keep the gurus in place, by agreeing to solve their problems and live by their rules.

Period.

Take a hard look, and know that gurus don't have to be any "smarter," or have any "experience," or do anything other than get agreement. (When I was a boy, "they" used to say that "anybody could be President of the USA." Today, after that brain-dead cheerleader and now our O-Bomber, I believe it.) And it's all down to agreement.

You've never consciously acknowledged that before. And you've never acknowledged the tremendous power that you wield with your agreement. Because you do have an unbelievable amount of power. Yeah, you as one "little man." The truth is that you can raise more hell with the "system" than you've ever imagined, if that's what you choose to do.

Why aren't you a guru?

How do you think new things come about in the big game? By magic? Do you think a hundred thousand people get the same idea at the same time? The simple truth is that one person stands up, announces the problem, gets agreement, and presto! a new game is born. And a new guru is on his or her way.

Take a hard look at the word, "experience." Look at it in relation to the business scene. You see advertisements all the time that say, "Experience required." That word is bullshit. It comes from the "HAVE ~ DO ~ BE" system. How many people would have gotten to work for Polaroid's Land if he ran ads which said, "Instant photo development experience required." Get the idea that way back when in every business, NOBODY had experience. SOMEBODY HAD A PROBLEM which others could relate to in their pictures, and they agreed to play the game of solving it. That's the way it was "way back when," and that's the way it is today.

HARD FACT:WITHOUT AGREEMENT, YOU'RE NOTHING. WITH IT, YOU'RE A WINNER. AND THE ULTIMATE IN AGREEMENT IS GURUISM, WHERE YOU GET TO DO NOTHING BUT HAND OUT THE PROBLEMS FOR OTHERS TO SOLVE.

Now let's take a look at idea-gurus. Take a Sassoon. Start with a picture reshuffle: "Your hair ought to look like this!" (Voila! the new style) You know what the first and only mandatory step is. After that, all the hair stylists go to work to imitate 'the look.' And the people right up there next to him in the Fifth Avenue salon have the opportunity to bitch that he really doesn't know any more than they do ~ and that he still puts his pants on one leg at a time. But he got the agreement, and he's the guru. And the agreement is all that makes him worth $250 to cut and blow you dry.

Without it, he's worth about as much as I am to snip your locks.

And how about Doc Spock, that reverent gentleman who sold two zillion books that instruct you how to raise a kid? Take a hard look: what did he tell you ~really ~ that you didn't already know? Could you have written that book? And now you get to see that the answer doesn't matter, because the truth is that the old Doc got you to agree to pay for those ideas, or he'd still be back in Boston with an office practice.

How do you think we got to the moon? Simple: you agreed it was a problem worth solving.

How do you think war games get started? People agree to play them, that's how. And that's all.

Next, a warning. Beware of the Agreement Trap. That is, the gurus of the world (and anyone else you agree with) can only get you to agree with WHAT YOU KNEW ALL ALONG.

And why is that? Simple again: Before you can agree with anything, you must comprehend it. Oh, to be sure, your pictures can be re-shuffled as I said earlier, but you must get the fact that they're just in a different order. Nevertheless, you had them on your videotape all along. And if you can't haul up the pictures from the past, the guy ends up being a ridiculous fool in your eyes, not a guru.

Next get the idea that the ONLY difference between you and the guru of the game is that he's at SOURCE, and you're not. You're playing his game, which means that he gets to make the rules, and hand out the problems for you to solve. And by your actions you agree that solving his problems comes before solving your problems and setting up your own games.

Don't you see that you're playing my game when you open and read this book? And that you already knew everything printed here? As you progress through the pages, reading the words, they must relate to your pictures, or you'd end up with complete nonsense.

And now you get to see that there's nothing "magic" about becoming a guru. And there's no "luck" involved either. In fact, the process is so simple, the true wonder is that it's eluded people for so long. To be a guru all you need to do is look and know if you're there. Then the only thing between you and actually getting there is space and time.

And that puts you at source in the game. You simply re-orient your life so that instead of waiting for someone to bring you a game, and seek your agreement to play, you're out in front, setting up your own games, communicating the problem to others, and getting them to agree to play. You've looked ahead, know where your river's going, what your purposes are, and then you simply set up your games to get you there. And you will intuitively know when someone or something gets in the way as you're going where you're going.

Get this: Gurus are always on the razorblade of choice. All along the way, you're going to have choices to make. Some will work out ok, and some will backfire. And you're responsible for ALL of them. So if you're slightly fearful of going out there on that blade, let me reassure you by telling you the truth: once you experience the game from the knife-edge, you'll never return to being unconscious, and backing into others' games. You'll really get a big grin when you see that your choices are working to get you closer to where you already are.

And you'll also get to be very calm and relaxed about your life. There's no effort involved. After all, you know where you're going. And you know where you come from. And all the hassles that people face who get themselves stuck in someone else's game, you get to avoid. You're setting up your own games, and you can literally have an infinite number of them going at the same time. And end up winning most, if not all, of them.

Hello, you guru you! Now you get to know that there are an unbelievable number of people out there, just waiting for you to choose where you're going, stand up and let them see that, and then you can begin to let them in on how to play your game. And then you get to hand them more problems. And they solve them for you. And you recognize them for that. And they're happy. And that makes you even more elated with the living experience.

By the way: that's all there is to the game called life.

8. THE FOUR BASIC (AND HERETOFORE SECRET)

"INGREDIENTS"

TO HEALTHY RELATIONSHIPS IN THE

GAME

The first thing I want to communicate to you with regard to relationships has to do with playing back some pictures of your past. Specifically, what I want you to do is look carefully at the unconscious world out there, and see the devices it uses when a declaration is made that a relationship is over. Done. Kaput.

What you'll see is that 99% of the people go about setting up an intricate game on the way to ending a relationship.

And it invariably involves establishing absolute wrongness for the partner. That is, they invalidate the other's act; cancel his vote, if you will. Then they get to walk away, and mutter as they exit: "Damn!, I don't know how I got into that in the first place. He/she was really an ass, and I knew it all the time."

It happens at the courtship level, it happens at the marriage level, it happens at the friendship level, it happens at the business level — in fact, if you look, you'll see that it happens almost all the time when a relationship ends between two persons.

The message I want you to get from this is simple: it is that what you're seeing is nothing but MINDS at work. Survival. "I've gotta be right!" So an elaborate game is created and played out which lets one "survive," while canceling the other's vote.

Look at the valuable time it takes to conceive, set up, and play out the invalidation game.

Point: any relationship you've had is simply back there on the videotape. Permanently. And you spent the time in that relationship of your own choice. Therefore, you can't change it, or get the time back. It happened. Let the thing alone.

So if you arise one morning and make a choice to exit a relationship, do it without canceling anyone's vote. Just tell the truth about it, without making the other person wrong. And don't wait a month, or a year, or a decade. What do you get out of sitting on a powder keg all that time? An ulcer, perhaps?

Now let's move on and talk about a good relationship. Healthy, growing relationships are rare in this world, primarily because people don't see what they truly consist of. And defining a good relationship is as simple as I, 2, 3, 4.

Good relationships consist of nothing but:

1. TOTAL ACCEPTANCE of the other person's river.

2. Actively creating games which FEED that river.

3. Creating a SAFE SPACE for the other person and having him or her KNOW that you will NEVER violate it.

4. COMMUNICATING with the other person about the three things listed above.

Starting at the top, with acceptance. This one is extremely basic. It has to do with complete understanding and acceptance of the fact that the other person is, indeed, on his own river ~ that is, has his own purposes, goals, ideas, etc. And when it gets down to those basic individual purposes, neither he nor you can change the direction or the flow. Oh, sure, you can try to push the river around, or get in the canoe and row against it, but you'd better get the idea that it's going where it's going, no matter what either of you decides about it. To push that river is equal to delaying the action. It's futile.

So, there's no change of basic purposes involved in a good relationship.

Just to be certain that you're clear on that point, I'm not talking about the "incidentals" in life ~ like leaving your clothes strewn all over the place, or always being late, etc. Those things you can successfully change, with no effect on the relationship. But at the nitty-gritty level, you'd better be at acceptance, if you want to be happy. And the "nittys" for you are the "nittys" for you. Look and know what your basic life purposes are. I can't recite them for you; I'm not you. This is a place where you can observe the unconscious world rowing against the river for a lifetime. Look around you — how many people are stuck in relationships when it's transparently obvious that they don't belong there? Are you?

The second criterion for a good relationship is where you can begin to see whether two people are really "getting it on" together. If they are, you'll see that each of them ACTIVELY FEEDS the other's purposes. Both of them create little games for the other to play that really turn him on, and they really enjoy seeing the other person doing his thing. Not many relationships are like that, but it is the unmistakable sign of a good and growing one.

Perfect example: the guy is relaxed and easy about his life; very informal. That translates to a preference for old jeans, a T-shirt, and tripping off to the mountains to wet a fishing line. She's into people, and affairs involving groups. The point is simple: if they expect to have a growing, healthy relationship, the first step is acknowledgment of the other, acceptance of those purposes, and then feeding the other. That's when a relationship is happy and effortless.

Creating a "safe space" for the other person consists of nothing more than expanding your space to include a corridor where the other can come in at any time, DUMP ANYTHING THAT HE/SHE CHOOSES, have you acknowledge what it is that's been dumped, and then JUST LEAVE IT THERE ON YOUR TAPE. Your partner must know (intuitively and implicitly) that you will never use that information as evidence against him, at any time, for any reason. Even when only the two of you are involved.

Sometimes the dumped material is called a secret, or it may be a confession, or whatever. The subject matter is immaterial. No matter what it is, if your relationship is getting better all the time, the other person will know that whatever was dumped will stay in the dumped pile. You may have a discussion about it, but you will never use it against him.

The final point is communication. If you're not talking, you're coming to the end of the line. Oh, to be sure, you can tie a "need knot" at the tail end and hang on desperately to that, but you should understand clearly what it is that you're doing. "Surviving,"and nothing more. It's the mind at work, serving you pictures of the past which keep you firmly stuck. And eons from happiness. You play that game; I'll save France...

Please note that I didn't say anything about need, or sex, or love. And I did that quite consciously, because they have nothing to do with the basics of a good relationship.

Take need. When you think you "need" someone, that translates to his/her ability to "do it to you." That is, if you need the other person and he isn't around, your life is screwed in some way, and he did that to you. And the person "needed" feels guilt, because he knows that he can't provide what's needed all the time. And the weight of the leaning person is especially heavy with the realization that total collapse is likely if he's not there to be leaned on.

What you must get is that you will survive, with or without the other person. You know that each of you has got your own river. Healthy relationships are a game based on feed, not need. That consists of creating little games to feed the other, and seeing little games created for you that feed yours. Now, *that's* where you want to be.

Thus, you can see why persons of the same sex so often have solid relationships. It's because they have the opportunity to deal themselves out of those games in the other's life where total acceptance is not possible. And, of course, to join in when they're together on things. Thus, no interference.

Let's not forget love. After all, it is what makes the world go 'round, isn't it? Maybe. I see love as a very simple phenomenon that all comes back to you. That is, you're either a loving person, or you're not. And if you are loving, then you're totally willing to give, with no expectation of getting anything in return. Therefore, another person can only get in the way and receive the love that you have to give. The point is that you don't "fall" in love — you're already there, or you're not. In relationships, love is the conscious choice you have when you look at another being, his river, the situation, and then you choose to let your emotions go. Add love to the basic four, and you're off to even higher ground!

Now take the time necessary to run some pictures of your past about the relationships you've had — and have. See what was going on. Tell the truth about what is (or was) going on. Look and know that a good relationship is an easy, effortless process. You're not fighting anything. You're not holding back anything. How good are your relationships? Wife? Lover? Parents? Kids? Friends? Business associates?

Next we'll take one paragraph and deal with sex. Sex is simple ~ it's another conscious choice you have, whether you like it or not. That means when you're hot, you're hot. If you've set up a relationship without the basic four, sex is just a frictional mechanism to cool you down. Add it to the basic four, and you really get to sail along in ecstasy. Because you will then get to see that sex is part of the other person's river, and you will communicate about what games are especially exciting to your partner. Then you proceed to feed those purposes by playing those little games. And, of course, you get yours set up and played out for you.

We're now at a point where we can discuss a phenomenon

in relationships which I call *pigeonholing*. The unconscious masses out there are doing something with people who come into their lives which is absolutely abysmal. It is that they never let the old videotape pictures alone. More specifically, when a person enters your life, you take the pictures of him. But then you store those pictures in a special place, and go back there and haul them up every time he re-enters your game. You've got him pigeonholed ~ stuck in those old pictures of who he is, what his purposes are, and how it all fits with your game.

Dammit, man, people change! Get the idea that every time you see someone, you're going to take NEW pictures. Seek out what's new for that person. Ask him about change. Spend the time putting a new episode on the tape. When you look through the camera of the present ~ each time ~ actively look for what's new and different about that person. Shoot new things! Stop locking people into your old pictures ~ you're wasting valuable film. And that includes those people you deal with every day ~ like your wife, your kids, business associates, friends.

Next I want you to become aware of the fact that the

unconscious masses use pigeonholing to fulfill new needs in their lives every time that need arises. Example: people have a pigeonholed picture which shows them exactly what a marital partner should consist of. How it got there is incidental ~ what's important is that it is there. And that they act on it. You see people who marry that "perfect" picture the first time around, split from it, but then (incredibly) they haul up the same flawed picture and marry it again!

Put your relationships against the true test: the basic four. And let the old pictures alone. They're in the past, where they belong.

Relationship games come alive when they're based on newness; freshness; exciting creations. No old pictures; the players get to see very clearly that they are where they are every moment of their own choosing. They understand that it's ok to change their minds. They see very clearly that they will only be in the relationship for as long as they choose to be there.

You see, the truth is that marriage is nothing but an arrangement ~ an agreement. It's not a goal, as so many unconscious people believe.

And now a word about who wields the power in male / female relationships. As I observe the game of life, I see that most of the time the woman has more power than the man. In fact, most men are basically chickens. You see, power in life is nothing more than the speed with which one can move his games from the BE stage to the HAVE stage. The less time spent in the DOing, the faster you get to have what you want. And I observe that most women are one hell of a lot less inhibited about taking those leaps than men. Perhaps it has to do with the fact that women have always been indoctrinated that they're "not that smart", so they can bumble more things and get away with it. Now, what a smart gal needs to do is to create a guy who's willing to accept and run with the power that she feeds him. Not many men are willing to take that power and use it, but they are in the game, if one is looking for them.

Another interesting thing, which I suspect is related to the reluctance of most men to accept the power that the gal has to give: it is that most women end up "holding back" some part of themselves in a relationship. It seems that they're hoping that some magic "knight" on a white horse will ride in someday and whisk them away into the legendary kingdom of happiness. First off, whoever you are, know that you put you in the relationship that you're in. Second, look and know that what is ~ really is. There are no knights left in the world — only the guy who trips in the front door every night. Why not give him all you have? Can you recapture that time? Can you edit it when it's over? Suggestion: You have a choice about remaining. And while you choose to remain, GET WITH IT. Be here and now.

We now come to the end of the discussion of relationships, with a look at a relationship that you have chosen to end. We've already looked at the methods most people use to get out: by being right, and making the other person irrevocably wrong. Canceling their vote. Act invalidation.

Now let's look at an example which clearly communicates what I want you to get. A friend of mine is living with a lady; they're not married. Now, he says that they both went into their arrangement with a clear understanding that it wouldn't involve marriage or children. Trouble is, he now finds that it ain't so anymore. She's begun to hint at the fact that it would really be nice to see the parson, and follow that with the patter of little feet.

He's looked long and hard at that notion, and knows he's not there. What to do?

Simple: the way to deal with terminating a relationship is to openly communicate about it, and not make the other person wrong in the process. The truth is that her river includes kids; his doesn't. Since that's really at the nitty-gritty level of things in the game, I would think that he wouldn't want to start rowing against his river in an attempt to stay even. It's time to separate. And the way to do that is simply to climb into her moccasins for a moment, acknowledge that, then tell her where you are. "Look, I understand that kids are really a vital part of you. You want them so badly that you can see them now. But I can't. I would really be misleading you if I went into that act, and ended up dumping you and the kids three or four years from now. So I want you to go out and find someone who's interested in kids, and have them. The time I've spent with you has really been beautiful. And we'll always have the memory of our lives together. But it's time to realize that we aren't going to make it from here."

Do you see what's happened? The truth is out, and it doesn't have to hurt anyone. Both of them will survive, and they can still be friends. They don't have to regret anything, or cancel each other. She can return anytime and share her new life with him. And he can really enjoy seeing how happy she is. And he gets to be happy too.

Life goes on. With no effort.

LOOK AHEAD. . . AND KNOW.

WHATEVER THE HELL YOU DO, DON'T ROW!

9. KIDS GAMES

This chapter can be very short — and not because kids aren't very tall. It's only because kids are human beings, just like you, and that makes them a part of the same game that you're in ~ the game of life.

Basically, your first objective in handling kids should be to get them to see that fact ~ very clearly. Now, you can set up fairy tales, or you can lay it on the line with them, but you must get them to see that they are really playing nothing but a game.

Ever notice how a kid responds when you say to him: "Let's play a game." It's natural to them ~ they really know the truth. So, when you establish the fact that they're in a game with you, and tell them what they have to do to win ~ they'll play along. With more fervor and enthusiasm than you ever dreamed possible. Using examples, you must get them to the place where they can see the game, and the fact that they set it all up. Also that it makes absolute nonsense to set up a little game, and then lose it. Get them to look ahead at both sides of the coin (theirs and yours) before they come to you and ask to play. Have them get the idea of looking and knowing whether the game they created is going to fly with you.

That's important, because if kids don't look at both sides, it's easy for them to become genuine pains in the ass. And that translates to them thinking that their games are the only ones in town. Then you get to lose.

If I were you, I'd tell my kids that my game is to enjoy life, and especially when I'm around them. So that when they get to be with you, they'd better set up the game to have you enjoy it, or they don't get to stay around for long. Take a restaurant scene ~(you know what those can turn into). Next time you go with your kids, set it up so that your game is to enjoy yourself, with them along for the ride. See how they can change their acts when the object of the game is to have you win.

In fact, I'd set up very few rules with kids. Because rules generally turn out to be concepts, and kids (like you) can't deal with concepts. They can only deal with experiences. For example, you could make a rule for your kid which says, "You can't ride your bike in the street." A youngster can't deal with that. It's there to be broken, simply because he knows that he can ride his bike in the street. ~ his ability there is no different than his ability in the driveway, or in the backyard. Now, in contrast, if you've had an experience with riding your bike on the street that you want to pass along, go ahead: "I rode my bike on the street, and got hit by a car." See ~ no rules. Or, "As I observe things, people who ride bikes on the street sometimes get hit by cars. And when people get hit, it's just when they think they're safe. Very few people get hit when they expect it." Still no rules.

Next I want to cite an exception to the "no rule" suggestion: make one, and make it this: TELL THE

TRUTH. Have your kids understand that you absolutely will not tolerate anything but the truth. EVER. And make it like gravity. You see, kids know not to buck gravity. Watch them ~ they come to the point of accepting it, and dealing with it. And that's the way you should be about truth. Like gravity. It's always there. And it's immutable. And you should be the most unreasonable, unpredictable human being alive when you encounter a lie from a kid. Believe me, he won't tell them for long.

Then get yourself out of the right/wrong game with your kids. Get to the point of acceptance of the videotape with them. So that when something happens, you should simply acknowledge the fact that you can't chase the tape and edit it.

Let's combine the rule about truth and your choice to get to acceptance with your kid, and look at an example: You awaken one sunny Sunday only to discover that someone's been up just long enough to have strewn the parts of ten different puzzles all over the bloody place. It's obvious who the culprit is, and it immediately gets to you, because you've already told the brat ten times not to take the puzzles out of his room. Again, stop and look before you go into vengeance (that old tape-chasing exercise you use so often).

What's your game? To get him to clean up the puzzle. parts? To learn from the experience? Then open with something like, "What's happened here?" And when you get at the truth, reply with, "Fine, I can see that. Now I suggest that you clean up the mess you've made."

Let's take the vengeance side of the coin and look at that. In fact, let's act it out. Get up out of your chair, and put you into the words that follow. Really get with it. Same situation: Puzzle parts all over hell's half acre. It's the tenth time it's happened this week. How many times do you have to tell the kid? So you walk up to him, wag your finger in his face, and scream: "IF YOU EVER ~ TAKE ANOTHER PUZZLE.~ OUT OF YOUR ROOM ~ FOR ANY REASON ~ I'LL BEAT YOU UNTIL YOUR ASS IS SO RED THAT YOU WON'T BE ABLE TO SIT FOR A WEEK! NOW CLEAN UP THESE PUZZLES AND GO TO YOUR ROOM UNTIL I CALL YOU!"

Stand up, right now, and scream that as loud as you can.

Great. What did you get out of it? Did you win the game? What game? Is anything changed?

While we're with that one, take a look at whether you want to have a rule in the house about taking puzzle parts out of their designated places. Do you really care where those puzzles are, or is it that you want your kids to be responsible for their actions?

Now you're getting the point. Just like you, the object with kids is a simple one: to have them SEE that they're CAUSING what happens to them. To get to the point of acceptance of the past; control of the present and the future. And to be responsible for their actions. All of them.

The final point I want to make about kids is that they already know where they're going. That they start out on their natural rivers and will stay there ~quite happy ~ unless you tamper with them.

That translates to you assuming the role of having your kids take a look ahead at where they're going; to ask whether or not they're already there. If they can look at you and declare that they already are, I urge you to let them experience that. Have them go through it. See if they really are. And you should observe what happens when you let them run their games that way. If it gets results, *keep it going.*

Get into the notion of asking kids flat out, "Have you looked at that? What's true about it for you?" Then take the time necessary to communicate with him about it.

Open the space in your game to allow a youngster to get into whatever he wants to get into. Urge him to wander into all sorts of new games, look at them, know whether he's a player, and then set it up for him to play. See if you can't expand your space to join him.

And if you see that he's stuck somewhere, get with the idea of communicating with him about it. Ask, "What is it [about your problem] that you don't see?" Be very specific with him. Get at the truth. And when you get there, be at acceptance with it. Then look ahead yourself for a solution. You'll be amazed at how creative you can be with a youngster's problem, once you allow for that problem to be real.

The result is that you'll see a young person who doesn't run his act on you. He'll get to see very early on that the object of the game is simply to WIN it. And you'll have a happy kid on your hands. Because he'll know where he's going, and that he's responsible for it, totally. And he'll see that you're interested only in feeding his purpose ~ which is to get him where he's going ~ as long as you can win too.

Then you'll get to see that you aren't "raising" your kid — what's going on is that you're *elevating* each other. And you get to be responsible for that. Totally responsible.

Next, you'll confront a choice: whether or not to love your kids. You will know that they're on their own rivers. And you will accept that. And you'll see that it's so easy to love someone who's riding on his river. It's true: the two of you get to float along together. With no effort involved.

Finally, you'll get to the absolute truth: That you CREATED the game called kids, and that you're winning that one too.

What else is there?

10. GAMESTUCK

OR

"THE TRUTH SHALL MAKE YOU UNSTUCK"

"Gamestuck" is a place you definitely don't want to be, at least according to my definition. And it warrants a separate discussion because so many people are, in fact, right there.

Gamestuck is exactly what the words say: people who are stuck in games that are either over, or that they clearly can't win.

And my message is just as simple and obvious: CLEAN UP YOUR ACT. Look and know whether a game is over or not, and if it is, close the game board, and move on.

Create another game, and play at that ~ to win. The truth is that you CAN CHANGE YOUR MIND. It's totally ok to do that.

Here's a clear-cut example we can share from our common experience: I call it the United States of America and the game of "frontiersmanship." That game consisted of "build like hell, just keep pushing on to new ground; putting up more new things!" In my view, it's now clearly over, but here we are, struggling to the last, trying to keep it alive. The result of refusing to acknowledge that it's over, close the board, and move on, is producing a disastrous mixture of events that have been well documented by the media — global warming, urban sprawl, pollution, new crime records, and the virtual destruction of a beautiful land.

Another example is Irving the Millionaire. As I told you, he rolled into the money station (where he was going all the time) with no effort at all ~ won that game~ but is now stuck trying to keep it going. What happened is the Company that bought him out proceeded to install all kinds of fancy new systems for him to use. And he neither agreed with, nor comprehended, what they were doing to his game. The fact is that when he sold it, it became their game, not his. He's no longer at source. And if he simply looked and knew that ~ acknowledged it ~ he'd move on, and keep doing what he had been doing all his life: being out there on the razorblade of choice, looking for what was coming down his river. Instead, he's now horribly stuck in what was; in an old game; one that's clearly over for him. And he's trying to make them wrong about what they "did" to his little company. Irving, clean up your act!!

Look at your games, and get at the truth for you. Look and know if they're going your way. And if they're not, close the game board, and move on to something else. Create another game, and play at that. Why do you insist on punishing yourself?

There are endless examples of this unhappy phenomenon in action. Look at the number of people who are stuck in relationship games that are clearly over. And instead of getting to the truth of the matter with themselves and the other person(s), then communicating that truth (without making anyone wrong, incidentally), they stick around. And try to rationalize what they're doing. How many times have you heard: "She needs me." Or, "We're staying together for the sake of the kids." Stop lying to yourself! The river of life goes on, and you're running out of film.

Look at all the business games that are run up frustration flagpoles for a lifetime. Those guys, buttoned down all day long, get unglued when they reach truth (courtesy of the Beefeater bottle), at the end of the day: "Man, I've got to get out of this rat race." And who do you see on the train the next morning, trying to row against the river?

If there's any sense to those games, I wish someone would point it out to me.

And I'm not suggesting that everyone's stuck in their games. What I am saying is that one hell of a lot of people are ~ and one good way to tell is by close observation. In other words, when you hear someone bitching endlessly about how the "world is doing it to me," you have a fair indication that he's stuck somewhere.

Clearly, some people are on rivers that are flowing with the commuter trains and the business scene, and they have grins on their faces. Some people are flowing naturally with the hippie game, the Junior League game, and on and on. Look at people's faces ~ you'll see what I mean. Get the idea that those who are floating along in their innertubes aren't trying. And then get the notion that for every existing game, some people are at source with it. They created it, and they get to hand out the problems, and make the rules. They're the gurus of the game.

What games are you playing? Yours or someone else's?

Look and know that the great unwashed masses are acting — trying to play. Hoping to discover the "secret" that will finally let them escape from the drudgery of going further downhill every day. Hoping (against hope) that "something" will somehow turn up that will let them enjoy life for once; relieve them of the weight of the sliding roller-coaster car they call their lives.

Now you know that there's no "hope in sight"; only help. And after that, one is faced with a choice: of moving up through a beam of light and getting to a condition called Acceptance, or of continuing to wallow around down in the Fishtank of Effect.

At the point of Acceptance, you look and know that the truth is that you cannot edit the pictures of the past, so you begin to run your life by letting them alone. Totally. You turn around and face forward. The password is, "What's coming?" The pointless question becomes, "What happened?" Unless you're running the tape just to look at it ~ and not in a futile attempt to change it.

When you really get with the fact that only you have the camera ~ and that the tape will never stop running as long as you're around, then you'll see that you want to control what goes onto the tape. Because you're responsible for it.

One additional comment about total responsibility: I want you to know that I know it's a rough place to get to. And the reason for that probably relates to the pictures of your childhood. That is, you were always able to "dodge" some portion of responsibility ~ however small ~ because you were "just a kid." And now your mind tells you to take advantage of that, whenever you can. It's easier than standing up and saying, "I am causing that."

Have you ever fully acknowledged the hard fact that you're on your own?

Are your parents still playing a game with you that allows you to skip the responsibility for some portion of your life, however minute? Are you still stuck there? Look at your life, and get at the truth of the matter.

It's not news to you that people get stuck in games like that all the time. And to get out of them is such a simple process. Start by looking at exactly where the other person is, and open with an acknowledgment of that. There is no need to make them wrong. Just tell the truth ~ not what they want to hear.

"Mother, I can understand that you care deeply for me. And I see that you still like to think of me as your little girl; all you've wanted is to be sure that I'm ok. But I've got my own life to live, and I'm going to go out and do that. And I'll be alright."

Or whatever the truth is.

Because you'll see, when and if you look, that the truth is a beautiful way to get unstuck from games that aren't working; that you aren't winning; or that are clearly over. In fact, it just might be the only way to get unstuck without making anyone wrong.

Look at the world and see how much time and valuable tape is spent by people spouting about one subject ~ when that's not what they have on their minds at all.

Like people who insist they want to talk about solving their sex problem, when it's the relationship that isn't working.

Or people who insist they want to talk about your relationships and how involved you are ~ when what they really have in mind is who controls your life.

Or people who talk about how right and reasonable they are ~ when what's really bothering them is that they're frustrated about losing all those games.

This is an entire game in itself that has a tremendous number of people horribly stuck ~ the game of lying to yourself. Of refusing to deal with the real issues as they come up. Of sublimating. Of "pretending" that you're not bothered by "it." Of "trying" to forget.

Get this: the truth is simply that lying doesn't work, and

that's the *only* reason you should junk it. And it doesn't matter whether you're lying to yourself, or lying to someone else. And it doesn't work because your mind won't let you get away with it. Oh, no, you got to "survive" by using it once, so your mind will store those pictures for you ~ whether you like it or not ~ and serve them up, again and again. So you get to build lies on top of lies, until you can't figure out what the truth is anymore. That's what I call a losing game. And the other option you've got is to go through the truth as it comes up. Acknowledge it. Accept it. Tell it to others. The hard fact is that you're doing nothing but wasting more of the valuable present when you lie. And you're committing yourself to wasting more time in the future, because the issue will be back to haunt you.

There's an old saying around from somewhere, and it happens to be bannered above the stage in my high school. The sign says: "The truth shall make you free."

In my view, that's not entirely true. You're already free. What the truth will do is get your mind and its "false survival" pictures out of your game. The mechanism is a simple one. It begins with the fact that you won't have your head in the sand anymore. You'll refuse to stand out there in the river on a rock, casting your fishing line backwards, trying to false-hook the truth in your old pictures. Oh, no, you'll be acknowledging the truth as it goes by in your life. Facing forward, with the breeze in your face, watching for the truth upriver.

And I don't want you to take my word for that: go and find out for yourself. My experience is that there's no feeling quite like the one you get when you get to the truth: You're the captain of the ship called you. You're setting the course, the speed, and you're out there on the bridge, steering. Not hiding below decks, even in a storm. Because you know where you're going. And you know that you're going to get there. And life is one of the easiest processes you have to encounter. You look forward to getting up every day, just to see what it is that you'll create.

And you know in your heart that you're as free as the breeze.

11. ONWARD AND UPWARD:

YOU'RE PERFECT, AND GENUINE

My closing message is a simple one ~ and not very original ~ "Happy trails to you, until we meet again."

My thanks to Roy and Dale, because that's true. Life is nothing but one happy trail if you go through the experience of doing what I've said here. Not around them ~ through them. Not talk about them ~ live them. No sublimation. No more lying to you, because the river called the present is always on the move. In fact, change is the only constant in life.

My purpose at this juncture is to tie it all together for you; to give you the absolute truth about life as I've experienced it, and as you will, in your way.

Let me begin by acknowledging that you are now in a space of uncertainty, in all probability. Uncertain about whether what I've said will work for you in your game. Uncertain about whether your life can, in fact, get any better. Uncertain about whether this book is "right," or whether a better answer is just around the corner.

First off, you should know that, "I don't know," is one of the highest conditions in the game of life. Especially when you're totally willing to be there. At that point, you get to see very clearly that you are at the crossroads, watching. And you'll discover that it's ok to be there. In fact, it's rather exciting. And you're also on the razorblade of choice; always willing to make one. No matter what it is.

So, my response to your uncertainty is: Fine. I understand how you feel. I've been there, and I must admit that it's not very comfortable. Here's what to do about that: Be very conscious about your life, for the next three days or so. Extremely conscious. Watch what's going on with you.

Go into your space twice each day (five minutes in the morning; five again in the evening), and take a careful look at what went on with you during the last 12 hours. Be conscious about your purposes. Acknowledge the things you've put onto the tape; be willing for them to be in the past. Get with the notion that you do have control of the present and the future.

Importantly, when you go into your space, take a hard, objective look at your life. Be truthful about whether or not it's working for you. And there's only one criterion for you to use in making that assessment: Are you winning the games that you set up?

And if you're not, now you're aware of the reason. It's because in life you end up with only one of two things in your games: the RESULTS you wanted, or the REASONS you didn't get the results. Nothing else. No in-betweens.

And when you fish for reasons, you're just wasting time. Because reasons equal RIGHTNESS. And rightness means that wrongness is also lurking. Which means that your mind is in the game, serving you pictures of the past. And that's what you definitely want to ditch. Forget reasons.

They're in the past, over which you have no control.

I really want to make this next point clear with you: the questions, "how" and "why," when you get to the hard truth of the matter, are unanswerable. That's because you truly won't know how or why when you're out there on the razorblade of choice. All you need to know is that your game is working better (or it isn't).

Remember the walking example? Remember also that, when you're about to go out the door, you intuitively know how to get there? And when something represents a "derail" to your purpose? Over time, you'll see that it's pointless to fish for reasons. Reasons just take time to find, and they serve no useful purpose at all.

You see, understanding how and why this world and your game works is not necessary for you to win ~ EXPERIENCING is what counts. Experience what's going on with you, right now. Acknowledge it. Forget the reasons; get the results.

Look carefully, and get this: People who are winning in the big game don't really know how they got there. Look at those people you call "successful." They don't know how they got there either. Oh, to be sure, they can (and do) make up all sorts of reasons for the Ladies Home or The Wall Street Journal, now that they've arrived. But, all along the way, they just kept choosing and being responsible for those choices. Look and know that they didn't "try" — it's impossible to "try."

Next, you'll see that a lot of successful people aren't really satisfied with themselves, or their new station in life. And there's a reason for that too. It is that it's not ok for them to be successful without knowing all the specific reasons why they got there. Said another way, they aren't at acceptance with the simple fact that they became gurus. It can really be frightening: if they don't know how or why they got there, it must be just as easy to knock them down from there! So they must keep seeking justification. And that's why they're not happy. The thing to do with that is the same as the advice I'm giving you: acknowledge what you are, forget the reasons, and enjoy it. Let it alone. It's back there on the tape. Move on to a new game.

Let me turn the tables on you for a moment: Suppose that

the entire premise of this book was that it is impossible for you to be happy until and unless you figured it all out. That is, before you could really enjoy life, you had to figure out how it all happened to you. And why it all happened to you.

Imagine the exercise of fishing for a plausible reason for everything that went on in your life. Every situation. Don't you see how pointless it is? Let the past alone. It just was, that's all. What do you choose NOW?

Next, I want you to take a long and careful look at your act. What are you getting out of it? (You are getting something.) Understand that, before you became conscious about your life, you were three distinct people. In fact, one or more of them may still be waiting to be cleaned up. The first person you are is the act you assume every day. You literally get up out of bed and 'put you on.' The next person you are is one who you're probably somewhat fearful of ~ that's the person you think you'd be if you were "natural" about things ~ if you junked your act. You probably see that second character as somewhat mean and unconcerned about others. Just generally nasty.

And the final person you are is the REAL you. And when you get to the real you, you'll find that you're beautiful. The real you is totally ok, and nice to be with. The real you is just fine. In fact, the real you may not be perfect, but you are certainly making *progress*.

The only trouble is that your "actor" phase put you square in the middle of the right/wrong game. That meant you could end up losing all the games you set up, but being ok about them as long as you were right. Now you know that being right truly doesn't matter ~ winning your games is what counts.

SO YOU CHOOSE TO GIVE UP BEING RIGHT, TOTALLY AND COMPLETELY.

Now when you set out with a clear purpose of being conscious about your life, you should understand that the characters and the situations will be the same. It's the outcome (results) that will be different, that's all. And those people who have been around you for some time will probably notice that you're playing a different game, and will ask what's going on with you. And you'll be honest: by communicating that you're not in the right/wrong game anymore.

And they'll get to see that it really is true for you. That you really do come from a different place. It'll be evident in your eyes, in the way you handle yourself, and in the general calmness and satisfaction you evidence in the game.

You should also get conscious about one more thing: that is, when faced with an issue, take the time required to stop ~ look ~ and consciously choose your course of action. If you must stumble or mumble, cough, or invent a body motion to allow you that pause, do it. Just be clear about your purpose before you take action. Remember that your mind is still there, desperately trying to make you survive. And if you're not conscious, it will serve up those pictures which it thinks will keep you doing exactly that. And that translates to making you right. Also remember that your mind desperately wants your life to be the same. That way, its pictures of the past are relevant to your "survival." The trouble is that your mind has now accumulated so many pictures for so many different events that, if you're unconscious, it serves up pictures for your entire game.

And that literally makes you a MACHINE. All you're doing is playing old pictures from the past.

Look carefully and really get this: when your mind is running your life by serving up "survival" pictures, you're on total automatic, just like a robot. If you let your mind plug in a set of old pictures, they have total and absolute control of all of your bodily functions, muscle reactions, feelings, emotions, attitudes, everything. When your machinery is running, you have feelings, but you do not feel. Those are pictures of feelings, not experiences of the moment of now. It's nothing more than an imitation of an earlier situation.

So, you must cut off your mind's automatic response. You must transcend it. In truth, you want to go out of your mind. And by being "out of your mind" I simply mean that you will stop ~look~ and then consciously choose.

The absolute truth is that life is a game of the real you versus your mind and its pictures of what it thinks constitutes "survival."

Be very clear about that last statement. Take a minute now

to look carefully at all the "buttons" you have. Those emotional triggers are nothing but pictures that your mind will immediately serve up in any situation which even remotely resembles an earlier one. These are the "loose wires" that can be plugged in, and they put you on total (unconscious) automatic until you run that act through. And, if you're not conscious, they can run your entire life.

I'm not telling you to junk all your buttons. No, I just want to make it clear that you're responsible for them. How many situations do you have in inventory where your mind has the response all racked up and ready to roll from the pictures of the past? What are the words I could say to you to make you come out of that chair, fists at the ready? What are the trip words that really upset you? Is there a subject you really don't like to talk about?

Look and know what your buttons are. Acknowledge them. You're responsible for them.

Good. Now, do you choose to let them run?

To repeat: get conscious of stopping, looking, and

choosing your course of action. And then, if you should

choose to go into vengeance in a situation, or anger, or hostility, or grief, or whatever, you will do that consciously. And you'll find that when you're conscious, the matter won't linger for a hour, or a day, or a year, or worse yet ~ a lifetime. Oh, no, you just go about cleaning up whatever it is that you choose to clean up, then return to dealing with the present and the future.

Because now you know that there are no mistakes back there on the film, only events which can be looked at. There's a clear difference: a mistake is something that has to be "fixed." You can't "fix" the tape. You can't tamper with the past. You can't edit it. You can't change it in any way, shape or form.

YOU CAN ONLY LOOK AT IT.

When you really experience that, you'll be at total acceptance.

And then you'll get to experience the fact that responsibility is the next natural station for running your game. And the reason for that is just as elementary: you'll see clearly that if you have any control in your life, it's only concerning the present and the future.

And when you're willing to be responsible for everything that comes into your life, you'll comprehend that you do have total control. Then, the problems begin to drop out, and your game begins to get progressively better. At first you won't believe it ~ you'll think you're just very lucky.

Over time, you'll know that it isn't luck at all. You will get to the place of acknowledging that it was no one but you who was "doing it to you" all this time. And that only you is doing it to you now. And that only you will ever do it to you.

And when you look at your life and know that it's working only because you made it work ~ that no one and no thing ever was or ever will be the cause of your life being whatever it is ~ you'll get the biggest grin on your face that you ever imagined.

And you can only go higher from there. Because the next thing you'll see very clearly is that you create your entire reality. You created the game called life. And you know that winning or losing is your only choice. And then you'll see that you really want to be a winner.

And then you are.

The truth is that, if you're running your act, you're doing that so that you ~ and all the others in your game ~ never get to find out who you really are. The problem is that power in life comes from being totally willing to be who you truly are, and to be totally responsible for you, and the reality that you create.

Look and know who and what you are. You DO know. You've just never acknowledged that fact to yourself before. And once you're clear about that, you'll be totally willing to make any choice, based on that knowledge. And you'll give up "trying."

You'll also be certain that no matter what you do, you will survive.

From here, you can build on you as high as you choose. As long as you open the space for that to happen. Just look and know. Then go. Don't row.

And there's no need to make anyone wrong in the process

of getting what you want in life. You'll recall that I said you create a "safe space" for others when you give up being right. And there's only one reason for you to create that safe space for others: it is that you understand that they are genuine when they express themselves to you. That's the truth for them. It's where they really are. And so, all you're doing is acknowledging their genuineness.

And you'll find that when your life begins to work exactly as you want it to, you'll be creating that safe space for everyone who comes into your life. You'll come to the point where you'll see that everyone is genuine and perfect. They're not lying to you. And it's ok with you for them to be where they are. Their position has nothing to do with whether you win your games or not.

You'll find yourself creating a safe space for mankind. For everyone. You will expand your space to include all of the people in your life. That's your world. That's the universe.

And then you begin to see that when you've expanded your space to include all of mankind, that you ARE mankind. Because you can only be what you expand your space to include.

And if all the other beings in your game are genuine and perfect, before too long it'll dawn on you that you must be no different. Then you'll see that it is that way ~you are genuine and perfect. Not a flaw in the real you. You, too, have really been where you've been all this time.

You see, when you're unconscious, you do whatever it is that you do in order to be "alright," to "survive," according to your mind. You have to be able to pronounce yourself ok, by justifying you. Now you get to see that you're alright ~ and will be ~ no matter what you do. It really is ok. You're beautiful. And you'll survive without any reasons. And you know that.

Then you'll get to see that you are the source. You create everything that comes into your space.

YOU KNOW ALL THERE IS TO KNOW.

YOU KNEW ABOUT WINNING THE GAME OF LIFE ALL ALONG.

* THE END *

EPILOGUE

THE BEGINNING

Just so we're clear at the outset, you've already finished this book. It's over. And you got your money's worth, or you didn't. This section is a "bonus" ~ just like that free bar of soap you get when you buy six at the regular price.

Because now that you've read the end, I want to take a moment to discuss the beginning. And of course, any discussion about the beginning has to be theoretical. So, this section is all theory ~ all "maybes" ~ this is the author's yarn about the beginning.

Oh! I should also mention that the secret of the universe might be revealed ~ but, again, I said "might be"; not "will be."

And before you read any further, please go and get a

dictionary. Any one will do. Just have it sitting there beside you. And as we wander together through this theory about the beginning, refer to the dictionary if you have any questions about meanings. Let's play that the dictionary is the "independent judge."

You see, there happens to be a great deal of truth in the dictionary, because it's been around for a long time, in one form or another.~ how else have we human beings been able to communicate with each other all this time?

Viewed that way, the dictionary represents an excellent historical device, because the words you see printed there have the AGREEMENT necessary to produce communication between two human beings. And both agreement and communication are the keys for us, as we shall see in a moment.

For now, I want to review some things, provide you with fuller definitions, and have you experience another exercise along the way. That's the path I've chosen to get you back for a look at the beginning.

WHAT ARE CHOICES-REALLY?

Earlier in the book, I told you that, in life, you had only two ways to get you where you're going: to CHOOSE, or to DECIDE.

And when you decide, you THINK that you must pick from the selection being offered at the moment. That's a lie, and it'll trip you up-badly, if you believe it, and act on it.

In contrast, when you choose, you know the truth: it is that your options, in the next moment of now, are LIMITLESS. Another word for limitless is INFINITE. That is to say: YOUR RANGE OF AVAILABLE CHOICES ~ RIGHT NOW ~ IS INFINITE.

You could choose to close this book, burn it, go to the airport, fly to a totally new place, and never be heard from again. You could, in the next moment, choose to scream, or eat ice cream. Someone could ask: "Would you like the radio on or off?", and you could respond by throwing a baseball over the left field fence. And, while it is also true that you may not consider some of your choices as very 'reasonable', that doesn't invalidate them, or make them "non-choices." It simply makes them available choices which you consider unreasonable.

Once again: the truth is that, in the next moment of now, your range of available choices is INFINITE.

IF YOUR RANGE OF CHOICE IS LIMITED — YOU LIMIT IT.

Don't read any further until you get that.

Experience it.

Just sit there, close your eyes, and begin to think of some of the things you might choose in the next moment.

Good.

Next, understand that the choices you INCLUDE in your available range in the next moment are yours, and yours alone. They come from you ~ they're your IDEAS.

Look up "ideas" in the dictionary. See that an idea is a "notion." Now look up "notion." See that a notion is an "inspiration," or (and better yet) a "clever contrivance."

So your choices are just notions; clever contrivances which you get and consider as "available" or "unavailable" to you in the next moment.

AN EXERCISE IN "NOW"

Before we can intelligently discuss the beginning, you must first see that your life "happens in" "occurs in," or "consists of" what I call "EVER-SUCCESSIVE MOMENTS OF NOW."

That is, your range of choices is, in fact, infinite ~ and is available to you in ever-successive moments of "now."

Close your eyes and click your fingers at the rate of approximately 60 times per minute, and experience your notions in each moment of "now" that occurs.

Experience the NOW! NOW! NOW!

Of your life. Do that. Right now!

Now let's take a moment and examine the experience you just went through. What was going on with you?

Well, when I do it, it's not long before I get bored. Imagine having to sit there for an entire day, clicking off 60 'nows' to the minute, and experiencing your notions as they occur. Shoot, it's no fun to do that, even if it is what my life really consists of! I want to be something; do something; have something.

Some other things were probably going on with you when you were conscious of experiencing 60 moments of "now" to the minute. Among them:

— YOU DIDN'T HAVE TIME TO PICK UP A POINT-OF-VIEW ABOUT THE NOTIONS YOU GOT. THEY WERE HAPPENING TOO FAST.

— THE EXPERIENCES WEREN'T IMPORTANT. AGAIN, THEY WERE HAPPENING TOO FAST FOR YOU TO ATTACH SIGNIFICANCE TO THEM.

— THERE WAS NO MASS, ENERGY, SPACE OR MATTER INVOLVED. YOU WERE JUST EXPERIENCING EACH NOTION AS A NOTION ~ AN IDEA ~ AND THEN YOU MOVED ON TO THE NEXT ONE. NOT ONLY THAT, YOUR EYES WERE

CLOSED, SO YOU COULDN'T SEE ANYTHING.

— YOU WEREN'T COMMUNICATING WITH ANYTHING OR ANYONE. YOU WERE SIMPLY EXPERIENCING YOUR NOTIONS IN EVER-SUCCESSIVE MOMENTS OF ~

NOW! NOW! NOW!

And so on..

So, to sum up: your life, in fact, "happens" in ever-successive moments of now, which, if that's all you experience, quickly becomes rather dull and boring.

Because you don't get to be anything, do anything or have anything ~ you just get to experience the "now" of it all. You don't have time for a point-of-view, or importances, or energy, mass, space or matter. And you don't get to communicate.

You just get to experience your notions as they come up for you.

HOW THE UNIVERSE WORKS

or

"WHAT'S YOUR NOTION?"

Earlier on, we looked at the "system" that the world told you about, and that you probably believed, and used.

It was the "HAVE ~ DO ~ BE" system.

And it says that if you want to BE something, you first gotta "HAVE," then you gotta "DO," and then, if you TRY (and get "lucky") you might get to BE "it."

And we also saw that there's nothing wrong with the world's system (that is, nothing's missing), it's only that *IT'S BACKWARDS.*

The truth is that the universe actually works the opposite way.

First, you look and know if you ARE.

Then you DO.

Then you HAVE.

We're now going to put a number of puzzle pieces together and take a look at how your universe works, in its totality.

First, I want you to be absolutely clear that your choices are limitless relative to what you'll be, what you'll do, and what you'll have, in the next moment of now.

And that those choices which occur to you will be simple notions ~clever contrivances ~ your ideas.

Next, understand that the notions you get are ABSTRACTIONS; that is, they have no matter, energy, mass or space when they are notions. They're just ideas.

Got it? If not, re-read it until you get it.

Good.

You are now ready to experience the NATURAL "flow" of the universe. Its "inner mechanism" revealed.

Here it is, in plain English:

BE is equal to your notions, your ideas, your choices, or abstractions. These are your EXPERIENCES; THE STARTING POINT.

DO equals the *construction* of them, the communication.

HAVE equals the agreement you get, and the concepts you create, in REALITY.

Thus, you can see that the truth is you get your notions BEFORE you construct anything, before you HAVE what you call your REALITY.

In point of fact, your ENTIRE REALITY comes from your notions. If you didn't have the notion first, "it" wouldn't be there.

And the KEY to your Universe is that you can choose TO BE AWARE that you're getting the notions BEFORE anything gets constructed; before you "have" anything.

Then, like magic:

You choose to construct ONLY those notions which will

serve your purpose. Those you consciously choose you then bring into (what you call) REALITY, so the smile on your face keeps getting wider all the time.

You see, when you were rowing against your river, it was simply because somebody else told you to "get this notion!". And you did. Then you constructed it as your reality, believing that the notion was yours in the first place. Trouble is (was), you KNEW that it wasn't yours, it was nothing more than what someone TOLD you. And you believed them.

The next thing to observe is another amazing truth: the SUBSTANCE of what you call REALITY is nothing but AGREEMENT.

Here's an example: I submit that you can't prove there was a "yesterday", unless you get agreement that it actually existed.

And the same is true of "tomorrow."

The same is true of tables, chairs, cars, and *everything else* 'out there'.

Without agreement, they don't exist in what you call reality. They exist at the EXPERIENTIAL level; as abstractions, but you *must have agreement* if you want to have them in your "reality."

Also notice that agreements are CONCEPTS. And you can't experience a concept. You can only experience in abstractions.

You see, human beings get in trouble when they "try" to resist what they have already constructed and agreed to.

They think that by *disagreeing* with a concept, it won't be that way anymore.

And that's equal to getting into a losing game with yourself. Because it's coming at it *backwards*, that's why.

Let your concepts alone. You already got the notion (unconsciously, perhaps, but you got it anyway) constructed it, agreed to it, and here it is, in reality.

Want to get out of it? Easy. Acknowledge what's so. Accept it. Take responsibility for it. Then get a new notion, construct that and get agreement.

Living example ~ The Generation Gap. Get this: I'm telling you that what happens between fathers and sons *starts* with the notion that the other is "unreasonable," or "dumb," or whatever it is that separates them. Then they communicate that notion (construct it), and both then *agree* that the other is an absolute ass. Then, sure enough, that's the way it is, in "reality." And, as a direct result, both of them get terribly stuck "trying" to resist a concept which they have already agreed to construct, and have.

Consider this as an alternative: How about one of them getting a new notion, something like: "Well, he is my kid, and I want to communicate with him. I think I'll get to know him a little better." Then *talk* to him about how you want to communicate. And see if you can get *agreement* in reality that both of you are ok.

Take wars. You get a notion of wars BEFORE wars exist, dammit! You *construct* wars. You *agree* to *have* a war, or wars wouldn't exist. Period.

Don't lie about it..

And *you* get the notion that your neighbor is a sonofabitch; *then* you go out and construct the sonofabitch, then you agree to fight with him. The point is that the sonofabitch wasn't "out there." Oh no: you got the notion first, and constructed him, and now you have him there, as real as all getout, and a sonofabitch, just like the notion you had.

You're responsible for *all* the 'sonsabitches' in your reality.

They came from your notions.

You're responsible for your reality.

Not "some" of it.

ALL OF IT.

You just weren't aware of it before.

Now you're aware of it.

Don't lie about it anymore, *if* you want your life to work.

You see, it makes no sense to RESIST what you've already agreed to. You can't change reality, because it *is*.

What you can do is be clear about your notions in each moment of now that you experience. And choose to "do" and "have" only those you want. That's exactly how you win the game.

And if something's troubling you now, it's probably the notion that you got a notion first, and actually constructed your PAST reality. It bothers you terribly to consider the idea that you brought all that "bad stuff" into your game in the past.

Get this: That's your mind back in the game, with its pictures of SAMENESS AND SURVIVAL. It's telling you that you were at EFFECT with the past; that you SURVIVED by REACTING the way you did, and that you will continue to survive ONLY if you keep your game the same.

And don't "blame" your mind ~ acknowledge it, accept it ~ and then choose to get it out of the way. YOUR MIND CANNOT CREATE ~ IT CAN ONLY IMITATE.

Now let's talk about your future reality. My notion is that if I told you that I had a "magic wand" which would let you create your future reality *exactly* as you wanted it, you'd buy it if you had to mortgage your soul. It's such a delightful notion that you'd give almost anything to experience it.

Well, you've got it.

IF YOU GET THE NOTION, AND CONSTRUCT IT THAT WAY, YOU'LL HAVE IT.

AND IF YOU DON'T, YOU WON'T.

One additional truth that tends to boggle the mind:

IT IS IMPOSSIBLE FOR YOU TO GET A NOTION THAT YOU CAN'T BE, DO OR HAVE.

If you got the notion, you're already there. You're already "it." At the *abstraction* level of experience.

And all you need to do to "have" the notion in your reality is:

~ Look and know if that's what you really want.

~Let the notion be OK with you, no matter how "unreasonable" it is. Said another way, COMMIT to those notions which you choose to construct in reality.

— STAY THE HELL OUT OF THE WAY. You will intuitively know what to do to have it.

You see, when your reality is DIFFERENT from your notion of what you wanted, it's only because your MIND got in the way and said: "You can't do that!" So you didn't.

Or:"That's not what they told you!" And you bought it.

Or: "That's not the same! Your survival is at stake if you do something different."

So you constructed the same reality that you always had. It's that simple.

Or: You said unconsciously: "*Maybe* it's ok for me to have that notion."

So your reality came out maybe. Maybe it worked; maybe it didn't.

Get that: Human beings are terribly reluctant to commit totally to their notions.

Because a commitment means that you're *wide open*= if you don't get what you want, you could be hurt badly. So you hedge your bet. You play "maybe."

You see, when your reality turns out DIFFERENT from your notion of what you wanted, it's only because your mind got in the way and screwed it up

Consider these examples:

—The man Jesus (before he became Christ) was a fantastic human being. He got some mighty miraculous notions~ let them be ok with him ~ and constructed them as his reality. Without trying. He got the notion to walk on water and just did it.

— "Faith healers" do nothing but tell people to "get the notion." Some of the people get it ~ let it be ok, and construct a new (healed) reality in their bodies. Others let their minds get in the way and stop the notion short of their reality.

It's that simple.

— The legendary "fountain of youth" lies in the acknowledgment of your notion of what ageing means. And up to now it reflected what "they" told you. So, you're getting older.

Man on the moon is a real reflection of a notion. A human being got it, communicated about it, got agreement, and we went there.

That's all there is. Your notions reflected in reality.

Another excellent example — the ghetto. Don't you see that the substance of the "ghetto" (like everything else) is AGREEMENT? Somebody got the notion of ghetto, communicated about it, got agreement, and there it is. And the kids in the 'hood' got told, "Get the notion that this is a ghetto, and you're stuck in it." And they do, or they don't.

You see, the ultimate message to people in (what you call) "bad situations" ~ like mental institutions ~ is to ask, "Why did you get the notion to be here, and then construct it? You know what you did to get here, and you know what you have to do to stay here. Or get out of here. Do you acknowledge that you had the notion? Do you accept it? Do you take responsibility for it? Good. Now! How long do you choose to stay in this insane place? How long are you going to stick with that notion?"

And now we're at the point of absolute truth:

RIGHT NOW, EVERYTHING THAT'S 'OUT THERE' YOU CONSTRUCTED FROM YOUR NOTION OF WHAT OUGHT TO BE OUT THERE. CONSCIOUSLY OR UNCONSCIOUSLY, YOU DID IT.

IT'S ALSO PERFECT, BECAUSE IT EXACTLY REFLECTS WHAT YOU WANTED.

YOU CALL IT REALITY.

AND IT IS REAL.

IF YOU DON'T BELIEVE ME, KICK IT.

AND IN THE NEXT MOMENT OF NOW, WHAT WILL BE OUT THERE WILL ALSO BE A SIMPLE REFLECTION OF YOUR NOTION OF WHAT OUGHT TO BE OUT THERE. YOU WILL CONSTRUCT IT, AND YOU WILL HAVE IT.

YOU WILL DO IT, CONSCIOUSLY OR UNCONSCIOUSLY.

AND IT, TOO, WILL BE REAL.

ALL OF IT.

AND YOU CAN KICK IT, TOO, IF YOU DON'T LIKE
IT.

OR YOU CAN TAKE RESPONSIBILITY FOR IT, AND
CHOOSE THE NOTION TO CONSTRUCT IN THE
NEXT MOMENT OF NOW.

You're ready for the ultimate trap of the Universe:

I TOLD YOU TO GET THIS NOTION:

THAT YOUR REALITY IS NOTHING BUT A
REFLECTION OF YOUR NOTION OF THEWAY "IT"
SHOULD BE.

AND YOU WILL EITHER GET THAT NOTION, OR
YOU WON'T.

THAT IS, YOU WILL EITHER ACCEPT
RESPONSIBILITY FOR YOUR NOTIONS
(ACKNOWLEDGE THAT YOU'RE AT CAUSE), OR
YOU WILL REJECT THAT NOTION (CONTINUE TO
BE AT EFFECT WITH WHAT'S ALREADY 'OUT
THERE').

IF YOU GET THE NOTION AND LET IT ALONE,

YOUR GAME WILL REACH UNBELIEVABLE HIGHS.

IF YOU GET THE NOTION THAT IT AIN'T SO, I'LL BETCHA YOUR GAME WILL BE THE SAME AS IT WAS.

AND THE TERRIBLE TRAP IS THAT YOU HAVE A CHOICE ABOUT THE NOTION YOU'LL GET.

BECAUSE THAT'S THE WAY IT'LL BE.

If you choose to experience life to the fullest, here are some suggestions about executing what I just told you:

1. DON'T BELIEVE IT.

2. EXPERIENCE IT.

3. BE CLEAR ABOUT YOUR NOTIONS.

4. COMMIT TO THEM.

5. STAY THE HELL OUT OF THE WAY ~ DON'T "DO" ANYTHING.

6. START SMALL.

Example: You get a notion to have a glass of water.

Look at it. Do you really want it?

OK. Then choose to have it, and have it.

The notion to get up out of the chair. Same thing. Look before you do and have.

The notion to go to bed.

On and on. Build from there.

Then go to your center, be clear about that ~ and choose to begin constructing it. Don't "try." You don't have to. Just commit to it. Communicate about it. Get agreement.

You're on your way to using the key to your universe.

And I'm just as happy as a lark that YOU got the notion to unlock the door.

WHAT'S THE SOURCE OF MY NOTIONS?,

or

"WHERE DO THEY COME FROM?"

An excellent question, and I'm glad you asked it. Because you're now ready to look at the truth.

And that simple truth will boggle your mind when you first read it, so I'll give it to you first, and then I'll explain it.

To review the question, so we're clear:

What is the SOURCE of my notions? OR:

"Where do they come from?"

Answer: The source of your notions is no thing (or nothing), and they come from no place (or nowhere).

Now let's move on to the explanation (before your mind

enters the game with its frustration pictures, and tells you to close the book).

The first step is to open your dictionary and look up the word, "nothing." Notice that the definition is:

— A THING THAT IS NOT ANY THING

— NOT SOME THING

Careful now ~ what we have is a thing that is.

It's just not ANY THING, as you know "things."

Could it be that we're talking about an abstraction?

A thing with no substance?

A thing to be experienced, as a notion, but not (yet) in reality?

And following that same notion, look up nowhere. Notice that nowhere is defined as:

— IN NO PLACE

— NOT ANY WHERE

Putting the two together, we have a thing that EXISTS (but not as a "thing" you can kick), and it exists in no place.

To repeat: The source of your notions is not a "thing" (or is nothing), and is not in any place (or is nowhere).

But now we have a small problem: If the source is (meaning it does exist), it's got to be located SOMEWHERE, right?

The answer to that question is yes, the source is located somewhere.

And in order for you to get where that "somewhere" is, I want you to replay your experiences from an exercise we did earlier in the book: the exercise in "now," when we clicked off 60 "moments of now" to the minute.

Recall that:

— Your eyes were closed, and you were alone, experiencing the "now" of it all.

— You weren't communicating with anything or anyone.

— You didn't have a point-of-view about your notions.

They were happening too fast.

— The experiences weren't important.

— There was no mass, energy, space or matter involved.

— It quickly became rather dull and boring to do nothing but experience the "now!" of it all.

And when you experience the "now" of it all, you experience the way it was in the beginning.

And the source of your notions.

Because you see, in the beginning, there was nothing. Nothing, that is, but you.

You were all alone back then. And you were no thing. And since you were no thing (or nothing), it follows that you were no where (or nowhere). Because when there was just you, how could there be an "up" or a "down?" A "high" or a "low?" In relation to what? There was nothing else.

You see, when you're all there is, you must be EVERYWHERE. Because nowhere is EQUAL to

everywhere, when you're all there is.

It is a fact that you must have at least TWO entities, in order to relate them, one to the other.

Theory is, that's exactly what you did. Once upon a moment of now, you were alone, just experiencing it all, without a point-of-view, without importances, and without time, energy, mass, space or matter.

And you got bored with that.

So you got the notion to play a little game with yourself.

That is, you said to yourself, something like, "Gee, this is rather boring. Wouldn't it be more FUN to COMMUNICATE?"

So you created a WORD game.

That's all life is ~ one big word game.

Don't lie to yourself about it anymore.

They even wrote it down, not long after the beginning. They penned:

"AND THE WORD WAS GOD."

Well, of course it was.

And you're "IT!"

YOU are the Supreme Being. In Spirit, that is.

And YOU got bored.

And you can get bored again. Close your eyes and click off 60 (or 120, or 1,200) "nows" to the minute. You have just re-experienced the way it is to be the supreme being.

Everywhere. ~ and nowhere. Nothing.~ and everything. No importances; no point-of-view. No time, matter, energy, mass or space.

And boring.

So the big game began when you got the notion to communicate. You also got the notion that communicating would be more fun.

So you created life/death, and human beings, with the intention of having them experience the human condition, and communicate with each other.

The truth is that you're NOT really a human being, you're

simply a Spirit BEing human for a time, that's all. And I'll bet that you'll give up that point-of-view, because I sense that the human will die, and then you'll just get to BE the Spirit BEing again.

The truth is that you're the SOURCE of everything; that the real you is an abstraction, not any "thing."

Your body is not you. Your body is simply a living expression of your point-of-view about the world. It reflects your notion of the way "reality" should be, just like the rest of the things 'out there' reflect that notion.

EXACTLY AND PERFECTLY.

Check this scientifically: your body (including your brain) TRANSMITS your notions; it is NOT the source of them. That is, no brain cell is the originator of a notion ~ they come from your source ~ which is you, the no-thing Spirit; The Supreme Being.

And you can get the notion that what I've said ain't so. In fact, that's what human beings have done all this time, and it is precisely why the quality of human life hasn't improved since the game began. (Notice I said 'quality,' and not 'quantity.')

You see, you get nothing but problems when you lie to yourself ~ because then you must continue to *defend* the lie.

Take the story of Adam and Eve: when I looked at it, I saw that what happened was that those two beings suddenly came to the hard realization that they had created the human condition. That is, they acknowledged the life/death of it; their mortality. And that realization scared the (proverbial) hell out of them. So they lied about it ~ refused to acknowledge that they had created the game called BEing human; and lied about the fact that it was a simple reflection of their notion. So they laid the CAUSE of "it" off on something else (God, if you will) and began to try to defend their human-ness.

You see, what happened was those beings simply FORGOT who they were and what they had done in the beginning, and began to think that they were their bodies. And who wants to die?

Fools. Because the next step was defense, and then the

MIND entered the game, in a desperate attempt to keep the body "SURVIVING."

Humans then proceeded to create different points-of- view about what constituted the best "survival" tactics, and then they got agreement, and formed groups. These groups marked off "boundaries" of defense, and then they formed "countries," had flags made, discovered gunpowder, and boom! the ultimate defense of a point-of-view is WAR, or "Survival of the Fittest!"

Look at that: we have killed untold millions of people in DEFENSE OF ONE LIE OR ANOTHER. (Side bar note: Charles Darwin disavowed his 'theory of evolution' just before he died.)

You see, there is no ethic in the game ~ really ~ until and unless you acknowledge the truth.

Which is: that you are the source of it all.

Example: Why would you get a notion, construct it, have it, then KILL it?

Example: When you create everything from a simple

notion, why STEAL things that exist?

Also notice that there isn't any 'right/wrong' ~ it simply doesn't make SENSE to be unethical.

Taking the other point-of-view, that there is a separate God who "caused" all of this: "He may not be looking, so I'll steal this thing, and worry about it later." Or: "This doesn't count. It isn't one of the laws I heard about."

Or, and even more absurd, assume there is no cause ~ no God ~ and that leaves you with a game of you against the world. The object is to defend, protect, and hack your way through it.

Look at all those people who think that they are their "collections." They have (literally) become their cars, titles, kids, houses, armies, etc.

Look at what absolute asses we've been, simply because we've been hiding from the truth.

And the truth is that the real you is no thing, or nothing.

If you're not willing to admit that, you end up with *nothing to hide.*

So you *act* like you're something.

Now, it's totally OK to act like you're something, as long as you know that you're really nothing. In fact, that's what makes the game fun to play.

Problems start when you believe you're really something, because then you get stuck in the losing game of defending whatever it is that you think you are.

And that brings us full circle; back to square one: YOU ARE NOTHING. DO YOU CHOOSE TO HIDE IT?

There's a fantastic playground out there in the world you created: it's called HAPPINESS. And in order to get in, there's an outrageous admission price:

THE ADMISSION IS NOTHING.

You see, life is an absolutely fantastic experience, when you live the truth.

And the truth is that the real you ~the Spirit~ had a point-of-view to express to the world when you created your body. Said another way, you had something to GIVE to the world. And here it is, big as life, called

_____.(fill in your name),

And if you choose to look and know what it is that you have to give to the world, instead of "trying" to get from it, you'll find that you'll end up with more "things" than you can handle.

And the process starts with looking at who and what you are.

You see, there's a lot of truth in some 'old sayings' that 'they' wrote down.

For example: "BE YOURSELF."

Nobody (in his right mind) ever said: "DO YOURSELF," or "HAVE YOURSELF."

Except the world, when "they" told you to get the notion that you were living in a "HAVE ~ DO ~ BE" system.

And you, you living, breathing ass ~ you bought it. And began to row in the opposite direction from the flow. You started to act from the notion that you "had to have" first, before you could "do" it, or "be" it.

The truth is that the universe works just the OPPOSITE way.

And THE ultimate truths are:

YOU ARE AT SOURCE.

THIS IS A WORD GAME.

"REALITY" IS A REFLECTION OF YOUR NOTIONS. TOTALLY AND PERFECTLY.

YOU ARE NOT JUST "BEING", YOU ARE *THE* BEING. SUPREME FOREVER; HUMAN FOR A TIME.

Sorry, there ain't nothin' else.

P.S. You are now "enlightened", as the Buddha would say, sitting under that tree...

WHEN DID THE GAME START FOR ME?

Another good question, because most people like to think that they get to climb off the responsibility train at the station called *conception*. That is, they come to the point of acknowledging that they are responsible for their past reality, back to the point where their parents got together, and sperm and egg joined to begin life's journey as the "you" you thought you were.

At that juncture, the control stick was "out of my hands"; "My parents did that, I didn't!"

Another lie that they told you. Let me clear it up. The truth is so incredibly simple that it (literally) stunned me when it came to light. First off, forget all those details about the union of egg cells with sperm cells. The point to get is the hard fact that you were ALIVE BEFORE any cells got together and formed what you now call you.

You had to be.

If your father slept with a dead woman (or vice versa), there wouldn't be a "you."

The fact is that those two elements were alive, and the result was another live thing. Forget trying to define the mechanisms. From life came life.

And that takes us right back to the beginning, when there was just you, experiencing the "now" of it all, as no thing, no where.

When you got the notion of life/death, at that point you came alive, as a *cell*.

AS A CELL, YOU'VE BEEN ALIVE FOR AS LONG AS THERE'S BEEN LIFE. IT IS NOT POSSIBLE FOR YOU TO HAVE COME FROM SOMETHING DEAD.

You see, as a cell, you've been occupying SPACE, you've been ENERGY, you've had MASS and MATTER, since you first got the notion and constructed those concepts. As a cell, you've been through it ALL. You set up the game, and you've been living it since the beginning. You've been on the time track since you got the notion that time would be a fun thing to have in the game.

That's why you have pictures of events you didn't experience in your present 'body.'

And you chose to expand your space, and come out in the body form you now occupy.

One of the most exhilarating experiences in life is the acknowledgement of the fact that you *chose* your parents. Of all the ladies and men around, you got the notion of who your parents should be, and you now have them.

You chose this day and age. You set it all up.

And all of it from simple notions that you didn't interfere with.

WHY DID I DO THAT?

Right off the bat, I want to acknowledge you for the way you phrased the question. It's very pleasing to see that you've gotten the message.

Because, as you know, most of the world is unconscious, and then they get stuck in the losing game of asking the wrong question, by crying out loud: "Why did 'it' happen to me?"

At this point I also want to reveal the SOLE purpose of this book. It is to get you out of the condition of FALSE CAUSE.

You now know it ~ and are willing to admit it.

And the "it" of "it" is simply you. You're the source.

Back to the question, "Why did I set up the game?"

I'm going to answer the question, and I'm also going to give you a bonus: THE "WHY" TO THE ENTIRE UNIVERSE.

You see, the answer to that question explains everything that's gone on with human beings since the beginning.

The answer to the question is the same one you can use for every move you make.

AND THE ANSWER IS: YOU GOT THE NOTION YOU GOT BECAUSE *IT SEEMED LIKE THE NOTION TO GET AT THE TIME*.

PERIOD.

STOP. RE-READ IT.

You now have the ENTIRE rationale for the past, and everything that's "back there" on your videotape.

You have ALWAYS been, done and had, exactly what it seemed like you should have at the time.

And you're trapped, because you WILL, in the future, be, do and have exactly (and only) what it seems like you should be, do or have at the time.

That's why your universe is perfect. And it's also why YOU are perfect, and genuine.

The "trick" (if you choose to call it that) is simply to become clear about your notions before you construct them, and have them in reality.

And now: will you please stop looking for "reasons," and go out and get results! I just gave you the universal reason, and one that always works.

And every human being out there is doing the same thing: EXACTLY, AND ONLY, WHAT IT SEEMS LIKE HE OR SHE SHOULD BE AT THE TIME.

If you acknowledge that to the people in your game, your horizons will expand unbelievably.

Experience this example:

Choose. Black or white?

Good.

Choose. Black or white?

OK.

Choose. Black or white?

Great.

Now: why did you choose what you did each time? If I ran you through that exercise about 50 times, you'd find that the ultimate answer (after you ran out of reasons) would be that you chose it simply because you chose it. No reasons necessary. It just seemed like the thing to do at the time.

You see, when you fish in your pictures for reasons, all you're really doing is spending more valuable time looking backwards. You can literally end up orienting your entire life against time. And the only thing I observe about that is that you're running out of time. You can see time slipping by. The answer is to choose what's right for the SPACE ~ and time will take care of itself. Choose for the moment of now that you're experiencing. Look and know. Choose.

It'll be ok.

It always has been.

THE GAME (Explained)

Throughout this book, I've referred to life as a game. And I've never told you exactly why I experience it as a game. Now I'm going to tell you.

Let's start with an example you already know about: Monopoly by Parker Brothers. Let's take a look at their basic notion ~ that is, why did they create Monopoly for you to play?

To be totally clear with you, I have not communicated with the original Parker Brothers to get their answer.

I assume, however, that what they had as the basic notion was for you to have FUN playing it. That is, Monopoly is simply something to do. The win/lose of it is not really important, unless you get the notion that it is.

You see, the truth is that there is NO INHERENT

SIGNIFICANCE TO WINNING OR LOSING AT MONOPOLY.

The same is true of life.

The truth is that EVERYTHING out there is simply a reflection of your notions.

AND NONE OF IT HAS ANY INHERENT SIGNIFICANCE.

IT JUST SEEMED LIKE THE THING TO DO AT THE TIME.

So, if some part (or all) of the game of life is SIGNIFICANT to you, you put that in. It wasn't "just there." You put the "charge" on it.

TO REPEAT:

THE TRUTH IS THAT THERE IS NO INHERENT SIGNIFICANCE TO ANYTHING YOU ARE, YOU DO, OR YOU HAVE.

THAT'S WHY IT'S A GAME. IT TRULY DOES NOT

MATTER WHAT NOTION YOU GOT LAST, OR THE

ONE YOU GET NEXT.

THE GAME JUST *IS*. PERIOD.

MONEY IS NOT SIGNIFICANT.

YOUR MOTHER IS NOT SIGNIFICANT.

THE WORD *SHIT* IS NOTHING BUT FOUR LETTERS STRUNG TOGETHER. (Besides, some folks call it 'poop.')

Since you created all of it, *none* of it is significant, UNTIL AND UNLESS *YOU* SAY IT IS. Unless you have a point-of-view about it. But it didn't start out that way ~ *You* put the importance in.

And I'm not telling you to drop your point-of-view. I'm just telling you that you're *responsible* for it. And that now you have another choice: whether or not to maintain the importance.

You see, the truth is that when you were no thing, just experiencing the "now" of it all, you didn't have a point of-view about your experiences.

You didn't have *time* for a point-of-view.

And when you stopped the process of experiencing, and got the notion to adopt a point-of-view, something else was born. It's been called EGO.

Then the point-of-view (your ego) must survive. And to survive *equals* being right, to your mind.

You will recall that your mind (i.e., your EGO) has only one purpose: survival of the being, or ANYTHING the beings considers itself to be.

Now do you see how it all fits? With a point-of-view about your experiences, with an ego, your mind then exists only to dominate. To dominate others, to dominate their points-of-view, to avoid conflicts that could upset your view applecart. Your mind thinks that your survival is really at stake. And make no mistake about it: the mind which finds itself defending a point-of-view will readily sacrifice the body in order to be right.

Consider the person who runs headlong into a burning building in an attempt to save some jewelry. A complete backfire of the mind.

Junk your mind. It is of no value to you in the game.

You see, your being-ness is what allows you to come alive in the game; once you get to the place of acknowledging that it's who you really are. Granting a "safe space" to other beings is to do nothing but to acknowledge their being-ness. It just is, that's all. Acknowledge your point-of-view, accept it, take responsibility for it, then just be there with another being. Don't let your point-of-view kill you ~ it has no significance whatever.

There's a simple summary of the paths we've traveled so far:

As the supreme being, you got bored with the no thing, "now" of it. You got the notion to be something, do something, have something.

So you set up this game, called life/death, and being human, for a time.

You had the notion that communicating would be more fun.

And you created all the rules.

So you're responsible for the game as it is.

All of it.

Everything that's "out there."

And it has no significance.

And you're *still* responsible for it.

And you get to be a player, because that's the way you set it up. You put yourself at dead center in the middle of a gigantic 'Monopoly' game, but the difference is that the board extends to infinity. You get to choose between the top hat, the cannon and the old shoe. But you have no choice about playing or not playing. Oh, no, you get to go around in the game called life.

Because *you* set it up that way.

You're IT. Choose.

It has no significance. Choose.

Life is one big "SO WHAT?" CHOOSE!

And since you're on the game board that you set up, you might as well create an outrageously good game from here. I'm telling you that when you get to ~ and through ~ "so what?" you'll find yourself in an unbelievable game: one called ALIVENESS. That's when you get to put *all* of you out there for other beings to see and experience, realizing that the here and now is all that is. Experience what happens when you junk time. Operate in the *space*.

At this point, you have the choice about maintaining all those "charges" you installed on all the buttons you carry around, waiting for someone to press, and put you on automatic. Transform you into a machine. Get with the notion that your point-of-view will die when it dies. You set up the life/death game. And the Spirit lives on. This life is but a (short?) stop along the way~

Now you get to see that you might as well go ahead and do all those things that *you* really *are*. Who are you bullshitting? There is no significance to any of it.

Hey, there ~ you in Cincinnati. Why did you set up the game that way? Is it your game? And forgetting all of that, what do you choose *now*?

And you, sitting there in Denver. Do you acknowledge that you put you where you are? And that you have a choice about remaining in that game. What do you choose now?

You're not trapped. Will you be there in the morning, and be responsible for whatever notion that you get? It will be a notion and only you will get it.

And you there in the war game, sitting on a sand dune with a gun in your hand. Do you acknowledge responsibility for the fact that you might get your head blown off? And if you do, you did that to you. You set it up that way. Who gets to win if you get your head blown off? What do you choose now?

Wherever you happen to be at this moment of now, get with the truth: that you are responsible for being there. And you're responsible if you get the notion to stay in that game, or to leave it.

Two more notions which deserve emphasis. First, you can now see very clearly that life is a series of "ANDS" ~ NO "BUTS." "But" is a reference to the past; "and" is looking at the next moment of now, which is the only place you can ever operate. And, that's the only reason you should "be here now." Now is where the (only) action is!

Secondly, the substance of the game is agreement. You

see, in order to have a game, at least two beings must agree that they will play. Otherwise, there is no game, just chaos. That brings us to the Old and New TESTAMENT. Did you know that a "testament" is a "covenant," which is an agreement? Look those words up in the dictionary. So we have an old and a new agreement. How 'bout that?

Enough of this. You now have the secret. You can "figure out" everything that's gone on since the time track started, if that's what you choose to do.

My suggestion to you is to get back to the present ~ the here and now.

And the next step for you is to get the notion that you will play from here on out for the experience of it, for aliveness.

Or you can choose to play for right/wrong, "survival" and domination.

If you choose to play as the simple being that you are, you will find at least four conditions there: health, happiness, love and self-expression.

HEALTH is much, much more than not being sick. Health is when you get out of bed each morning at the same time as that body you chose to inhabit, not two hours and three cups of coffee later. It's the feeling that a great day is coming, and you want to be conscious to experience it. You want to see, hear, and be there with your creations. You'll get up with live anticipation and excitement for what's coming. And you also get to give up the need to "wind down" at night, after spending 3/4 of the day "jacking yourself up."

HAPPINESS is the knowledge ~ and note I said you'll know it ~ that you're perfect, that you set up the game, that the game has no significance, and you acknowledge it, and ALL OF IT IS OK WITH YOU. And all other beings are perfect too. You set them up. And that makes the world a fantastic place to be ~ to experience ~ because here you are, creating it. You can even grin about it. You do have one helluva game going out there, don't you? Kinda funny you were that creative about it, huh? Ah, c'mon, you knew there was nothing significant about it all along. Life just is, that's all. Get with it. Sit there a minute and really let that sink in. Then gimme a big belly laugh! ("A man who can laugh at himself will never cease to be amused!")

LOVE is when you look and know that you are just a being, and that you created all the other beings in your game. And then you'll remember that you do love other beings. And you've loved them all along. You see that we're all part of the same game, and it's absolutely fantastic to be able to relate and communicate and love and express your beingness to another being. That's what you had as the notion when you set up the game. You got screwed up because you forgot that. You picked up a point-of-view about your experiences, and you allowed your mind to enter the game and defend that point-of-view. But now you get to experience the perfection of other beings, and love them because they are spirited beings, just like you.

Next time you're with someone, just be there. Look beyond the body, the mind, the conversation, and see his being. Experience that being. That's life. That's living.

SELF-EXPRESSION is what you will experience when you become willing to simply put you out there for other beings to observe. Fully, totally and completely. Forget the fear that you've always had about being right about what you express. It has no significance. *Tell the truth*, and see if that works. Remember that you are not your expressions; you are the being. Put your expressions out there to the other beings, and let them alone. COMMUNICATE TOTALLY FOR ONCE IN YOUR LIFE. WHAT PURPOSE IS THERE IN "HOLDING BACK?"

If you're upset with the game you've got going, create a new one. But there you are, of your own choice, in the here and now. You might as well get into it, because you did choose to be there, consciously or unconsciously. And it's ok, because everything you did seemed like the thing to do at the time. The tape's running: what do you choose now?

You'll find that you create other conditions when you come alive in the game: one of them is that you get to experience your emotions again. All of them. Those that were trapped in sublimation or fear; those you "clipped short" when you didn't want to expose the real you. Those you sat on when you felt they "weren't acceptable for an adult to show to the world." Let them out! They have no significance either. Put them on the line. Experience the feeling of knowing that the truth is out there, and you did that.

You'll also experience energy, and it'll seem like it's boundless. It'll be coming from the knowledge that you created the whole thing; that you're responsible for it, and you accept it for what it is. Then you'll really want to experience more ~ faster. You'll get to experience all the good things you've missed all this time. And your game gets better every day, when you see results.

Next you'll give up those electrical charges and all the buttons you've carried for so long, and you'll create *enthusiasm*. You'll know that the future will be totally ok, because you will create it, and it will have no significance. So you might as well grab life and living while it's there to be gotten. YOU GET TO CREATE, AND CONSTRUCT, AND HAVE THE NOTIONS. THAT'S ALL THERE IS.

And finally you'll get to *inspiration*. That's when you go "out of your mind" ~ literally ~ and return to just being and creating. You sit back and see all this ~ what a beautiful, crazy, wild, unbelievable game you set up, and that you're responsible for, and you acknowledge that.

Then you can totally create your reality. You'll see your true purposes come to reality for you. Just like in the fairy tales, except that this one happens to be called your life.

Look carefully, and let this one sink in, because it really is the key: In the game as you set it up, you have only two choices about how you'll get where you're going. The first is the unconscious method, where your mind will create your reality from your pictures of the past. And you know that it is most ready and willing to do that ~ in fact, that's the only reason it exists. But you should also know that it can only duplicate earlier situations: IT CANNOT CREATE. In fact, your mind cannot accept the notion of creation, nor can it accept the notion of disappearance.

So, that's your first option: to let your mind run you as a machine, and keep you "surviving."

The only other option you've got is to become conscious of your notions, by letting your being come forth and set up your reality. And that means you'll be out there on the razorblade of choice: always willing to make one. You'll begin to constantly look forward as your game progresses; watching the truth as it becomes reality.

Get this: You are going somewhere. That is, in a week, or a month, or a year, or ten years, you will be somewhere. What I'm telling you is that you're going to CREATE where that is, either with your mind and its pictures of the past, or from your being. That's the only choice you have in the matter. And what I'm suggesting is that you should consider the desirability of being conscious about your notions, and stop bitching about them after they get to reality. There's nothing "accidental" about them: you will get them, construct them, and have them.

Of course, the game works both ways. When you create an upset for you, you did that. And when you create a pleasant thing, you did that too. And the object of the game is for you to score more "wins," whatever a "win" is for you. And to lose fewer games as you progress, and your creations get better and better.

Begin to carefully watch what happens to your reality when you become conscious about creating only the notions you really want to have. Then commit to them.

I would also suggest that you give up the creation of SYMBOLS, and start creating EXPERIENCES. And the reason for that is simply this: you can't ever get enough symbols if you've never had the experience. That is, no amount of money, jewels, friends or anything can be the experience of happiness, security, love, or of any experience. The experience of any of those things begins with the knowledge that you are just the being. No thing in the beginning, and a spirited human being for a time. When you acknowledge and accept that ~ truly ~ only at that point can you proceed to enjoy all the symbols.

Toodledoo, my friend. And if you're getting the notion that a "thank you" would be the thing to do for me about now, please forget it. You only get to thank me when I do something "to" you or "for" you. And I didn't do anything to you ~ you KNEW it all along. I told you that in the introduction to this book. You got NOTHING from this book, and I want you to be absolutely certain of that. You just got me to put the words down, that's all. And you get to take responsibility for getting the notion to open it and read it. And I'm just as happy as a robin in Springtime that I created being here with you in your game.

Just play nice from here on out, will you?

Oh ~ one other thing, lest I forget. I love you.

And that is the beginning.

SUPER BONUS: HOW IT ALL FITS

As I observe things "out there," what I see is that each of us, at the time we chose to become human, came into this life with only a few basic notions that we wanted to have in reality. In my view, these are (not necessarily in rank order), as follows:

TO BE HAPPY

TO BE LOVING

TO BE SELF-EXPRESSIVE

TO BE HEALTHY

Let's face it, if you had all of the above in your reality, what more could you ask for? When you really get down to it, what else is there? Would everything else you needed *come out of these*?

Take a look at that.

Good.

Next, let's look at what actually happens with most of us. You start out with the notion of becoming a happy, loving, self-expressive and healthy human being.

And (since 99.9% of the world is unconscious) chances are you chose unconscious parents. And you went to them, looking for happiness, love, someone to express yourself to, and for your health needs.

Since they were unconscious, however, and hence didn't know who they were, or what the game was all about, what you ended up with is people who could hardly be expected to GIVE you their love, or even some part of it, when they were desperately trying to get and hold on to all the love they could.

Allow you to express yourself? They had the notion that they had to keep quiet about things, so where do you get off as a six-year-old that you can speak out?

Be happy all the time? Now, dammit, you and I both know

that some rain must fall! Jeezes, kid, will you be *reasonable*?

So you ended up with little or no love, self-expression or happiness. And then you began to get sick every once in a while.

The next step was very logical, when you found yourself running up tunnels with no cheese: You got the notion that those basic notions you started out with weren't genuine. That is, you saw that when you committed to having those notions in your reality, you got only frustration, and it hurt like hell. So you shut down the notion that your notions were the cause of it all.

And since "they" were telling you what notions were ok for you to have, what it was ok to do, what things were ok to have, you began to look to "them" for your next notion.

You see, you simply shut off the notion of being at cause with your reality (which is the way you started this whole game), and began to be at effect with it.

Then you started to say "Alright, what's the next notion? What can I be? What can I do? What can I have?"

And you let "them" tell you.

The only trouble is that "they" didn't look and know either. They just proceeded to tell you what someone else had told them. They believed it, and so did you.

They said something like: "All I know is that it's a tough world out there. And if you want to survive in it, you had better get the notion that money is the thing to collect, so you can buy lotsa food, and a better house to stay warm in, and get this and get that, and get all you can while you can!"

So you've become one helluva collector. I'll bet you've got more "things" (stuff) than you can count.

And you're probably ready to defend every one of those things.

Well, try getting this:

THE TRUTH IS THAT YOU'RE THE SOURCE.

And what can the source do?

When (and if) you get to the truth, only one thing: **GIVE.**

GET THAT: AS THE SOURCE OF EVERYTHING, THERE'S ONLY ONE THING YOU CAN DO ~ AND THAT'S GIVE.

The truth is that you're putting out BEFORE you get anything back in your reality.

And if you're putting out "hate," I'll bet that you're getting plenty of it back in your reality.

And if you're putting out "scarcity," I'll wager that things are scarce for you, in your reality.

And you're doing all of it simply because it seems like the thing to do, given that you've come to believe that you can't satisfy your basic human notions. When you went after them way back when, you got only frustration and blind alleys. Then you lied to yourself (unconsciously), and said "Aw, I really didn't want to be happy, loving, self-expressive or healthy in the first place." So you began to take "their" notions, and do what "they" told you to do.

"They" said there was a mysterious God who caused all of this, or "they" said there wasn't. And you bought it. You said.: "OK, I got that notion." So there was a God for you, or there wasn't.

There's only one fairly large problem with that: it is that you are now heading toward actually becoming the "they" of "it," and very fast. Which is to say that, at some point in the future, people will be saying "They say (fill in the slogans.)

And you will be the one who created and communicated what it is that "they" will be saying about the way "it"is.

It used to be "They say you're at effect with it."

It could be: "They say you will choose what's next for you ~ your reality will come from your notions. And you will be responsible for it." The truth is that we humans are not creatures of circumstance ~ we are in fact *creators of circumstance*!

That's such a horrible trap it'll take you a couple of days to absorb it fully. Starting right now.

Let's keep going with what you created as you progressed through your life to this point: Having shut down the validity of your own notions, and begun to do what "they" told you was ok, you found that it was a hell of a lot easier to just follow their notions most (if not all) the time.

And some smarter-than-average humans figured out that what you wanted was to be told what notions to get. They're called "gurus."

They get to tell the tales, you listen, and agree, then construct their notions as your reality.

Your boss says: "Show up at 9 AM. Lunch for an hour at noon. Quit at 5. You'll get $477 per week." And you agree: "OK, I got that, and I'll do what you say."

And if you get really good, you get to tell a whole bunch of people (millions, even) about your notions at the same time. And get them to agree, then construct them in their reality.

Look at that marvelous electronic wonder = television. Can't you see what that mechanism does? It simply says: "OK, get the notion that the thing to do is watch this program called (fill in your favorite show) for the next hour."

And you sit there, constructing the program as your reality. And at commercial time, the sponsor gets to tell you: "Get the notion that the way to have more friends is to use my soap/toothpaste! mouthwash/deodorant, etc."

Now you can see that McLuhan said it all when he said: "The medium is the message."

Sure it is. When human beings are unconscious, it literally doesn't matter what the program is saying, as long as the notions keep coming, I don't have to create my own. Which leads to sameness, survival, and minds in the game.

Do you know what the "creative" department of an advertising agency consists of? Simple: people who get the notion that it's ok to have their own notions, and to construct them in reality. They're the ones who actually get paid to write the ideas that end up on film in the commercials you see every day. And they get to think up all those soap opera dramas you watch on the tube.

The point is that they get agreement that they're "creative." Then it becomes ok for them to get ideas, (within certain commercial limits, naturally) and communicate those ideas to other human beings.

In fact, in and out of ad agencies, the better you get at agreement and communication, the more money you'll make, if that's what you choose to pursue. That is, the more people you get to agree with you, the more successful you become.

And the point for you is a simple one: Do you choose to follow someone else's notions? Do you choose to do what "they" tell you? Do you choose to have what "they" say you should have?

First off: WHO THE HELL ARE "THEY?"

You see, if you've been unconscious, you probably have the notion that it's totally ok for you to create headaches. So, as a solution to your problem you get to choose between Bayer, Anacin, Bufferin, Alka Seltzer, and whatever else "they" have to offer.

Because that's what they told you you had to choose from.

And you bought it. You're buying it, by the millions, every day.

Now tell me this: What the hell is the *difference* between telling you to choose between all those remedies, and telling you to choose between headaches and no headaches?

COULDN'T "THEY" GET ON THE TUBE AND TELL YOU TO JUST PLAIN CHOOSE?

Instead, they chose to get on the tube and tell you things like ~ "there's a recession going on."

Dammit, don't you see that the SUBSTANCE of a recession for YOU is your AGREEMENT with their notion? And until you agree, it doesn't exist? Recessions get constructed, like everything else you have in reality, from some human beings' notion, followed by agreement.

And they don't exist without it.

A recession gets started when some human, somewhere, gets up one day with the notion that "things look dismal to me." And he communicates that notion to another human being. Let's pretend that the recipient is the editor of a major newspaper. He hurries to the press room and sets a headline which says: "RECESSION ON ITS WAY." And then millions of people ('sheeple'?) read the paper and agree: "Boy, they say things are gonna be down. I guess I better not buy that new car this year. Better wait and see what 'they' have to say next about the way it'll be."

A recession consists of nothing but an ever-widening circle of agreement.

Same with a "boom." Agreement, nothing more.

How do you think the stock exchange works? Do you think the prices appear from some magical source? Sorry: the truth is that someone gets the notion "General Motors is gonna be up this morning." Then someone else agrees, and the opening bell reflects their agreement.

When you become clear about the mechanism, you'll then be free to ask yourself: "How long will I follow their notions? What is my notion?"

Look and know whether you're CHOOSING to be what you are from the infinite range available to you; whether you're CHOOSING to do what you're doing; CHOOSING what you have.

If you're not, don't bitch. The only reason is that it's not ok with you to follow your own notions. Which is another way of saying: when you have a complaint, go to someone who can actually do something about it. GO TO THE SOURCE.

And you're IT. Always have been.

Don't you see that the inventors of the world are simply people who get notions, then commit totally to having them realized? They start out with only an idea, and with no thing in their reality. They simply know they'll get there, that's all. And agreement is what makes it real. End of the mystery about inventors.

You see, this discussion is leading us nowhere but back to square one: YOUR CHOICES IN THE NEXT MOMENT OF NOW ARE INFINITE.

You could choose to abandon every thing you have. And then do something else. And all you have to do is look and know. Then go.

Example: Let's assume that you chose to pull the plug on your TV set, cancel the newspaper, and simply go about your game without experiencing what was going on "out there."

Question: Would a depression *exist*? Would the stock exchange exist? And, ultimately, DOES ANYTHING EXIST, EXCEPT WHAT YOU EXPERIENCE?

Well, as I observe things, you have chosen to be aware of your experiences through a 'thing' you call your body. Thus, what you experience as an alive being is EXACTLY and ONLY what you experience as an alive being.

And you chose NOT to experience your aliveness through a tree, a dog, or me.

Which is another way of saying that what you are, what you do, and what you have, is every-thing that IS, for you.

Look! I could dredge up all kinds of facts and tell you about them. A couple of examples:

** 1,017 people actually die every day of the dread "Dogears" disease. However, you don't experience that.

Does it exist?

** 17 people climb Mt. Keystone every week, just for the hell of it, and along the way they step on (and crush) an average of 46 flowers. You choose not to experience that, either as a notion, or in your reality. Does it exist for you?

** 746 cars are made every day in this country without a rivet in the socket that holds the widget in place which could affect the brakes. You don't experience that: you're not aware of it; you don't make those cars, and the one you have happens to have the rivet. Does the problem exist for you?

First of all, I want you to be clear that any of these "things" could become a genuine "cause" for you ~ if you chose to have it that way. You could choose to go out and demonstrate for your favorite cause.

And the point is that all of them (plus an infinite number of additional examples) illustrate only one simple fact: if you don't experience it (either in reality or as a notion)

WHAT THE HELL DIFFERENCE DOES IT MAKE WHETHER IT EXISTS OR NOT?

Which just happens to be the answer to that age-old Zen

question: "What's the sound of a tree falling in the forest with no one around?" Simple: "The sound of a tree falling in the forest WITHOUT ME AROUND is the sound of a tree falling in the forest without me around." Period.

What you must get is that you have a choice about your notions in their TOTALITY. That is to say, *you* choose to move your notions from the way they start out ~as abstractions ~ into construction, then into your reality.

You have the power to take a concept (like a recession) from the notion stage on into construction, and then you have a recession in your reality. Or you don't. And that's all there is, for *you*.

When you acknowledge that ~ truly ~ you will see that two simultaneous things happen: As the source of it all, you have the most incredible power you could ever conceive of, and you're using it every day. Your reality is the evidence for it. You'll also discover HUMILITY, because that power can certainly be misused.

Which is only to say that ALL OF IT starts and ends with you. So, if you choose to create an absence of wars in your reality (or to experience wars only as a notion, an abstraction), you will then choose not to *do* anything to construct a war, and you will never *have* a war in your reality.

And every other human being out there has the same choice about his reality ~ including wars, recessions, and everything else ~ whether he's aware of it or not.

There's an old saying I heard once that is very relevant here. It goes something like:

"It ain't what you *don't* know that gets you into trouble.

It's what you THINK you know that ain't so."

Get it?

You should take a look at THINKING and what you're doing with it.

While you're at it, take a look at BELIEVING what you don't experience.

Then look at HOPING and see what you do with that very convenient device you created.

Maybe you will choose to junk them all.

Then you might choose to look and know who and what you are (and *only* you know), proceed to *do* that, and *have* that as your reality.

And human beings who LET GO and simply experience life that way, as I observe things, usually end up being happy, loving, self-expressive and healthy.

Take a look at what *you need to let go of* ~ that is, what notions ~ that are between you and being happy all the time. Could you be healthy all the time? What's between you and CHOOSING that, right now?

What notions do you need to let go of in order to GIVE the love that you have? Could you be loving all the time? What's between you and choosing that? What if we define 'love' as the simple willingness to give to a person, place or thing, with **no expectation** of getting anything back in return? Can you live (and love) with that?

Letting go of the notions "they" told you about, and creating your own.

That's precisely what *aliveness* is all about.

You see, in my view, the sole purpose of life is to acknowledge that you're the SOURCE, then choose to be the character you know you are. It'll all flow naturally (just like a river) from there.

Some wise soul said this, a long time ago:

"To Be Or Not To Be..."

A THEORETICAL CONVERSATION IN SUMMARY OF WHAT WE'VE LOOKED AT

Reader: "Ah, c'mon, Frederick, this book is nothing but your point-of-view about the way 'it' is."

Author: "You're right. And, as I observe things, as a SPIRITED human being, you are stuck with having to choose a point- of-view too.

That makes me and you = the same.

As long as we're alive.

So what will your point-of-view be?

And do you acknowledge that you will CHOOSE it, from an infinite range of options?

And do you acknowledge that, from the point-of-view that

you will choose, will come *your* reality? That your point-of-view will be the cause of the reality that you create?

Which is another way of saying that there's NOTHING out there in the next moment, and won't be, until you create it.

And it'll be created from your notion of what ought to be out there.

FINALLY!

Don't you see the mind-boggling way it can be

When we get human beings

To create reality

Responsibly?

And with that notion, may I simply say:

"Goodnight, Dick."

As the curtain closes, it is well to remember:

Conscious people (those at SOURCE) talk about their NOTIONS, their IDEAS.

Mesmerized (TV/computer) people chat about EVENTS.

And *Unconscious* (fishtank folk) mumble and grumble about other PEOPLE.

Let us commit to remaining conscious!

ABOUT THE AUTHOR

Carl Frederick is a free, spirited, individual, All-American, bestselling author, world-wide adventurer, green thumb gardener, fly fisherman, practical philosopher, goodwill ambassador, and at the present moment, a willfully dispossessed vagabond, trudging the spiritual path to a happy destiny, planting Mother Earth's seeds and random smiles, all along the way.

Perhaps you will meet him, out on the trail, where he is, ever so slowly, turning pro..."

www.carlfrederick.org

###

Made in the USA
Middletown, DE
17 October 2016